John Paul Stuy

NEXT DAY TRAFFIC

The Secrets to Effective Automotive Marketing

JOHN PAUL STRONG

AUTHOR OF
Next Day Traffic
A SERIES OF BLOGS

NEXT DAY TRAFFIC
The Secrets to Effective Automotive Marketing

© 2015 John Paul Strong

First Printing, 2013

ISBN: 978-1-62620-498-0

Printed in the United States of America

TABLE OF CONTENTS

Preface 1

Chapter 1 | The Three Types of Traffic 3

Chapter 2 | The #1 Source of New Business................................11

Chapter 3 | The Contents of a 30-Second Commercial................19

Chapter 4 | It's That Time of the Month…Every Month 27

Chapter 5 | Price Sells Cars...35

Chapter 6 | Cash Cars Are Constant and Retail First Rules..........43

Chapter 7 | The Four A's for Holiday Months 51

Chapter 8 | Hot Traffic Solves Cold Merchandise 57

Chapter 9 | Spikes and Dips 65

Chapter 10 | The Five Types of General Managers........................73

Chapter 11 | The Easiest Traffic to Drive: Service Traffic 83

Chapter 12 | Clean Up in the Service Lane 97

Chapter 13 | Connecting the Dots 111

Chapter 14 | The Smartest Internet Guy in the Room 121

Chapter 15 | The Perfect Storm of Traffic 129

Chapter 16 | Price and Online Merchandise 139

Chapter 17 | Buying Sponsorship Versus Buying Leverage 147

Chapter 18 | Glory Days 155

Chapter 19 | Momentum 163

Chapter 20 | 10,000 Missed Opportunities 171

Chapter 21 | A Terrible Thing Happens Without
Promotion…NOTHING 179

PREFACE

"A DEALER ONCE TOLD ME..."

Those five words are the foundation of this compilation that focuses on the precepts and processes necessary for generating the lifeblood of every automotive dealership in the country – next day traffic.

Since beginning my chosen career in retail automotive merchandising over a decade ago, I have visited hundreds of dealerships and spent countless hours in dialogue with some of the most successful business-savvy operators in this business. During that time, I observed both dealers and upper-level managers who just could not get their heads around everything necessary to drive shoppers to the dealership or website.

Whether our dialogue was insightful or bordered on "what the hell are you thinking?" I made it a point to always take meticulous notes which I then put into journals for future reference. This discipline was a lesson from my father, Mike Strong, who in building his illustrious reputation always said, "Find out what you don't know before you tell them what you think you know."

I am grateful for all who shared their knowledge and personal experience in showing me what is necessary to sustain and achieve growth in this competitive arena. My objective for writing this book is very precise in that it presents tools –not theories – when applied and executed with accountability, have proven to produce traffic while avoiding costly errors.

During the time of writing this statistics reveal that shoppers physically visit only 1.4 dealerships in the buying process. My hope is that you are the "1", but if you aren't, I hope that this book gets you there. I love this business for many reasons, but something that has always stuck with me was a dealer once telling me about the exhilaration he enjoyed after exceeding a sale's forecast.

1

THE THREE TYPES
OF TRAFFIC

There is only one thing in the retail automotive business that I have found all dealerships have in common: Every dealership, regardless of the franchise or location, lives and dies by its traffic. Traffic could be the most misunderstood word by people in the car business today, but this chapter will set out to clearly define the very essence of what traffic is and, most importantly, where traffic comes from. I have used this phrase many times with a firm belief in its truth, "I have never met a problem in a dealership that couldn't be fixed with traffic."

Traffic is critical for any business, but for businesses that only sell large ticket, low-turnover items traffic can be defined as immensely critical. Traffic is the difference between a dealership being profitable and poised for growth in the market, and a dealership bordering on bankruptcy or losing its franchise from the manufacturer due to poor performance. Dealerships that do not attract, generate or maintain traffic are most commonly the dealerships that have low consumer opinion and terrible online reviews. Why is this the case? Very simple: Dealerships that are not able to compensate and effectively manage top-level talent will never be able to completely satisfy their customers and will not be able to remain a great place to do business. They go hand in hand; dealerships that lack traffic almost always have the highest industry turnover because nobody wants to work there. And if they do work there, it's usually not for very long. A dealership that always has traffic will most always have good employees, and thus the effects of it trickle down throughout every aspect of the dealership's operation.

Traffic is important in the good times, when the industry is experiencing record growth in new and used vehicle sales and the sun is shining on our economic model. But traffic is the single greatest asset any dealership can have when the economy is in turmoil (like in the years since 2008). The ability to effectively find and generate traffic in this market has been the reason for my company's growth and it has earned us the reputation of being on the very forefront of automotive marketing and advertising. There are not a lot of companies in any spectrum of the automotive industry that have tripled in size and grown their profits over 500%—but ours is one and this book will tell you why.

To understand traffic, you must first understand where exactly to find it in the retail car shopping process. Too many dealers and marketers do not know where to look for or how to find today's buyer, and they have a hard time telling the difference between an ordinary shopper and an actual buyer. This is also one reason that the general public gets so annoyed with ads from dealers that appear to be obnoxious or seem too good to be true. Most people in our industry do not understand that every retail ad should be crafted just like a blueprint for a house. There are elements needed and elements that should never be included. Knowing what to leave in and what to leave out comes directly from understanding who the shoppers are that you want to reach.

I like to use a funnel to illustrate the retail buying cycle as a visual device. It illustrates how people filter down as they get ready to buy a new or used vehicle. A person enters the buying process at the very top of the funnel. Buyers are first exposed to the following items as they start the process:

- Category Awareness
- Brand Awareness
- Ad Awareness
- Message Association

As people enter this top category, they are determining whether they are going to buy a new or used vehicle. Are they buying a car, truck, SUV or van? Are they buying import or domestic? Are they buying from the same dealership or person they bought their last vehicle from? Are they going to pay cash, lease or finance? All of these factors start to play into the equation as a person first enters the retail automotive buying cycle. And a large part of the awareness process steers the shopper in one of many directions as they start to move toward a true selection process.

Once somebody has made it through the first tier of shopping, they really focus in on the exact brands that are on their shopping list. This is like going to the grocery store knowing that you are going to buy beer but not knowing which exact brand you're going to purchase. As people transition through this process they are commonly exposed to the following items:

- Brand Imagery
- Brand Consideration
- Brand Favorability

As people study and do their homework on these brands, they will begin to see one brand take the place of another based on personal preference and factors that they deem are the most important. During this phase people will consult third-party sources, vehicle shopping websites, blogs, reviews, and magazines like *Consumer Reports.* They may also ask people about their level of satisfaction with the chosen brand. Once people have narrowed down their final choices to one key brand, they have their heart set on it. And they are now ready to flow downward to the very bottom of the funnel.

Welcome to my world! I have lived the last 10 years of my life right between the area of purchase intent and the actual purchase. This is the very essence of where the traffic you should be going after lives and how you should be talking to them. There are only 3-10 days between purchase intent and purchase to convince the buyer to buy from you. When they are this far down the funnel, you are directly staring down people who are about to make the final decision on one of life's major purchases. When you think about how narrow the timeframe is, it can almost be shocking, but it makes total sense. I am only interested in finding people who are going to buy a specific make and model of vehicle in the next 10 days because these are the people that will create the most and immediate traffic.

Throw the idea of long-term marketing strategy out the window—I am looking for next day traffic. I am looking for people who have already made up their mind not only to buy a vehicle, but are going to buy the vehicle that I am promoting. That is how you narrow in and drown out all the other noise in the marketplace. That's how you determine exactly what traffic is and what type of traffic that you want to be talking to.

Now that we have clearly defined what traffic is, I am going to break it down into three types. The marketing approach is slightly different for each type. The first type of traffic is what I call "natural traffic." Natural traffic is the easiest type of traffic to find and will always be the likeliest to find you. Every automaker and franchise outlines their dealers by location based on geography. Within this geography, every dealership has some type of assigned area that their manufacturer tells them is their responsibility. In some cases, but not all, these assigned areas are pretty well mapped out and equal to my area of natural traffic premise. As I see it, natural traffic is defined as the shoppers who are going to put you on their shopping list because your store is in an area or on a specific road or highway that this person travels or is very familiar with. Natural traffic is the traffic that is going to shop with you at some point in their buying process simply because you are convenient to where they work, live or go to school. This type of traffic generally results in a higher than average purchase rate because the dealership is the ideal place for them to buy in terms of location.

If a retail automotive operation is run right, managed right and conducts good business, then there should be a relatively high conversion rate among its natural traffic into buyers. It is very rare that we see a dealership or an organization with all the right working parts and processes that isn't able to hold the largest share of their assigned area by converting their natural traffic.

The second type of traffic is called "owner body traffic." I tell people that I do not care whether you took a high school economics class or went to Harvard Business School; you will always learn, "The number one source of new business is the person that you are currently doing business with." Owner body traffic is the greatest source for new business because it continues an existing relationship. This comes mainly in two forms: either by repeat purchases or through referrals. I have found that most dealerships do not communicate nearly enough with their owner body. And even if they are communicating with their owner body, they are not going out of their way or spending the money to provide effective communications and compelling reasons to do business again.

Your current base of customers will typically provide two things that you do not see from any other type of traffic. In most cases that I have studied and reviewed, previous customers provide a greater margin for the dealership as they are not shopping or buying based on price alone. People will pay a little more when they know they are going to be taken care of and the service will be there after the sale. The second thing that previous customers almost always provide is a better customer-satisfaction rating or CSI as deemed by the manufacturers. It has become very important in the last decade for this industry to rid itself of the bad perception. When conducting repeat business, these customers are generally going to rate you higher because the level of trust already exists.

The third and final type of traffic is "created traffic." It is because of created traffic that I, and most independent advertising companies, have a job in the retail automotive environment. Created traffic is when you take your advertising budget and spend it so that your message is shown and delivered to viewers who are right in between the purchase intent and purchase section of the funnel. Oftentimes, created traffic will come from areas that are not within a dealership's assigned area. The sole intent of pursuing created traffic stems from finding people geographically that might not have shopped with you in the first place. The premise behind this form of traffic is that they were most likely going to buy from another dealer, but were diverted because we knew how and where to reach them with a message that spoke to them at the perfect moment in their buying cycle.

Created traffic can also be called "second-shot" or "third-shot" traffic because in many cases this form of traffic has already shopped one or two other retailers before they found you. Finding created traffic is important because it increases sales volume and market share but generally does not generate as high of a margin as natural and owner body traffic. If not managed properly and margins are not as profitable, it can be a negative factor for a dealership, but the positive aspects almost always outnumber the negative. If retailers were to truly break out their advertising cost per unit sold and take into account what percentage of their business either came to them naturally or through a previous relationship, they would be appalled at the amount of money spent on generating fresh traffic. It would surely cause some people to not advertise or promote at all, because the cost to generate traffic becomes astronomical when looked at from this perspective.

Most advertisers and dealers do not break out the differences in traffic in accounting for the dollars they spend, but it doesn't change the fact that there are only three ways that traffic is going to find a dealership. People have theories about all different types of campaigns or unique methods of generating traffic, and some of those will be addressed later, but when it comes to traffic, this is the very basis of how to define what it is and where it comes from.

This premise holds true for advertisements placed in any form of media. Whether the ads appeared on broadcast media, online media, direct mail, direct contact media or even something as simple as the newspaper, traffic comes to a dealership from one of these places. Once this premise is understood, a dealership can begin to focus on the areas where they can benefit the most. Dealerships have varying factors that impact them in several ways, just like any business, and it will live and die by its ability to understand the three types of traffic. They will use advertising dollars to speak to one of the forms of traffic living between purchase intent and purchase in the buyers funnel.

2

THE #1 SOURCE OF NEW BUSINESS

As I said earlier, I find myself telling people all the time, "I don't care whether you took to a high school economics class or graduated from Harvard, the most basic foundational lesson you learn is that your number one source of new business is the person you are currently doing business with." This premise and philosophy has been used in our industry over the last 30 years to generate tens of thousands of retail car sales from dealers in every state. This is a lesson and practice that is at the very core of any effective marketing plan. The real kicker is that I do not just tell people this for their business. I use it as my golden rule in building and cultivating my own client base through the use of referrals and existing customers.

The number one source of new business for you is the person you are currently doing business with. They already exist, have already had the experience, and they know the good and bad about buying a vehicle from you. A comfort level has been created due to their previous experience. The size of any owner body is going to vary with the size of every dealership. Some dealerships have a larger service business than others, so in terms of the sheer number of previous customers, they may exceed the average because they have built a larger base over the years by servicing more vehicles not directly sold from the dealership. On the flip side, some stores may have a higher rate of sold vehicles than service vehicles because they operate a more aggressive front end, have a higher volume product, or may be a destination point. Regardless of the nuances that make up a dealership's owner body, the typical dealership that has been in business for any number of years should have several thousand—if not tens of thousands of customers who have either bought or serviced from that dealership. When you start to do that math, the numbers and calculated return on investment really start to make sense.

Take for instance a dealership that has been in business for 10 years and has 20,000 sales and service customers housed in its customer data files. If there are 20,000 unique customers and at any point you figure that one percent of this customer base is in market to buy a new or used vehicle, then there are approximately 200 people who have done business with your dealership in the past who are thinking about buying another vehicle. When you start to estimate monthly sales goals and the cost to go to market with an effective plan, the amount of business that can be created from your existing owner base is daunting and it is right there for the taking.

What many people in dealerships have a hard time understanding is that their greatest source of new business is sitting right in front of them. These previous customers are buying every day. Generally one percent is estimated to be in the market at all times and is going to be doing business in the next three to 10 days.

Existing customers are without question the most overlooked new business prospects in a dealership's business model. Part of the challenge for most dealers is that there's no exact marketing plan or precise tactics on how often previous owners should be contacted or what message will cause them to respond the most. There are a lot of theories and opinions on what aspects of direct marketing and direct contact will generate the greatest traffic counts or sold-unit counts, but this is the one area of retail automotive marketing that lacks finite principles and set guidelines. The real kicker of it all is that this should be the most effective source for new business and is the most underutilized. The way to combat this is to build a marketing plan that allocates enough resources and dollars on a monthly basis to send out communications to your previous customers to generate a response that results in new business. This is a simple premise and concept right? Wrong.

Multiple decisions must be made before a plan or strategy can be applied. I have broken it down into five points that, regardless of franchise, size or dealership location, must all be addressed and decided on before a plan can be created.

1) What's the Size? The size of your owner base will be the greatest factor in determining the amount of effort and dollars it is going to take to effectively market. Once the total audience is determined, you can apply the frequency of how many people are contacted every week, month, quarter and year to effectively market to them. Once the frequency is applied to the audience size you are reaching, you can get a very accurate picture of how many of these people will be in the market by assuming that one percent are always ready to buy. The size of your owner base is also a true representation of the size of the market that is ready to buy. In other words, some weeks and months will show more activity out of the existing owner base because there are more people buying that week, while other weeks will show less people. Dealership owners and operators oftentimes do not understand there will be ebb and flow in this audience. They remove their focus from marketing to the owner base when times get slow or after a slower than usual patch. The focus must always remain on targeting these customers regardless of any ebb and flow in the response. If you do the math, there are buyers who have bought from you before who are getting ready to buy again. The bigger the owner base, the more people you have to talk to who are about to buy at all times. Do not be on again and off again. Analyze the size and establish a plan so that you are constantly talking to your owner base about buying a new or used vehicle.

2) What's the Message? The message that gets sent out to the owner base is one that I have probably spent about half of my life defending and discussing. This falls into the category of, "everyone has an opinion, and some are better than others." No two stores are the same and thus no two stores' client bases will be the same. Since there are so many differences, there can be some alterations based on the needs and wants of the people who will be receiving the message. If a store, as previously mentioned, has a larger base of service customers than sales customers, this store would greatly benefit by sending out direct mail and email that is skewed heavier with service offers, coupons and daily maintenance specials. This store has a greater percentage of owners who will respond based on needing service. It provides a way to remain at the forefront of their minds once they get into the market to buy. On the other hand, if a store historically has greater sales volume than service volume, their messages would need to be aimed at pulling more sales customers forward than trying to market service. The greatest point of all in terms of a message is that no message is a bad message. Every mailer or email that gets sent ultimately makes an impression, and by making an impression you are already winning the battle for mental shelf space with the customer. The bottom line is: The message should always be sent and it should be created by knowing what a customer base is most likely to respond to based on the structure of the dealership.

3) How's It Sent? I always instruct that the way a message gets delivered will vary a little by each dealership. Right now, there are three highly effective ways to target your existing owners. The mailbox, email and telephone are the most tried-and-true, effective forms of outwardly marketing to the masses and generating the greatest response. Every American has a mailbox. Some have more than one, and it has to be checked even if a person doesn't like to get mail and sorts it over the trash can. With the proliferation of the Internet, email and online bill paying, both people and businesses have made the move to do more communicating electronically than through the standard U.S. postal system. I for one, couldn't be happier with "less mail" being sent now verses five years ago. Less mail coming into a person's home on a daily basis allows your mail message to stand out and make more of an impression than it would have five years ago. Making an impression in the mailbox costs money for printing and postage, but it is about the only form of marketing that allows you to place a physical item in someone's hand.

Email is another valid—and more cost-effective than direct mail—way to talk to your owners. The latest data shows that 94 percent of adult Americans have an email address. Most dealerships have not done the greatest job collecting customers' email addresses, and generally find a lot of them to be out of date. But once an email base is established, you can market to it at low to no cost because the only expense is the manpower to send out your notifications.

The final and absolute most critical form of sending the message is the telephone. Telephones are the lifeline of any business—especially any dealership. If the phone is not handled properly, you could have a customer who says they will never do business with you again. The phone can be used to notify existing customers of programs that are too important to be left to mail and email notifications. The phone can be used when an offer, service or program is so amazing that the dealership is compelled to take the extra step of notifying people with a phone call. The real barrier keeping more dealerships from being effective with their previous customers via the phone is manpower and execution. Unless a business development center or outside call center is established, many dealerships are not able to execute an effective outbound phone-calling program or system through their general sales department. Phone systems can be highly specialized and difficult to manage, but if done right, it will have the greatest response of all in generating new business from existing customers.

So with the three main ways to reach existing customers, every dealership must decide, based on their size, budget and ability, which ones are going to be used and at what frequency to cultivate new business from old business.

4) How Often? This varies based on the manner in which the communication is sent but recommended timing is as follows:

- **Email** – can be sent two to three times per month. Many mass-targeted emails are caught in spam filters or deleted if a person is not interested at that moment. This means more can be sent but the response will be less. Because of the ability to send out multiple messages each month, these messages can vary from sales and service to general information about the dealership or a special event that is going on this month.

- **Mail** – can be sent every 30 days or set to send every 60 days if the customer base is too large to contact all owners each month. I believe in mailing previous customers every 30 days whether they buy from you each month or not. The mailbox is just like a TV in that it is a channel that allows you to make an impression. The customer will still see that you sent them something, whether they choose to act on it or not. With all the money spent to spiff salespeople and on other advertising methods, I think the biggest fallacy in our industry is not mailing your owners enough.

- **Phone** – can be used three to four times per year. This should be used sparingly as it is the most intrusive form of outbound marketing. Calling to provide information or occasional updates is different from calling every week and trying to sell something. Customers who are cycled through a calling program need to be monitored very closely as to not anger or frustrate them with your efforts. It can be the most effective form, but can also hurt you the most if not done correctly.

5) How Long Do You Do It? The easiest answer of all—forever. Once you develop a system to mine your existing owners and outwardly market to them for new business, you never stop. Sure you will have some campaigns that are more successful than others, but remember this is generally a function of the size of the target that's in the market. As you grow your dealership's business you are constantly selling and servicing more vehicles which means your owner base will expand over the years. As it expands, the trade cycles and buying habits generally don't change that much, you'll just find they buy different things. This is why it is of dire importance that you develop an effective process and plan to always be in front of your current owner base. There will always be the need to track your success and make refinements in your program. If you see that service penetration among your owners has increased and your repair order counts are growing on a monthly basis, you may need to increase the effort of your marketing to sustain this increase. On the other hand if you see that your return on investment from sales has decreased over multiple months, you may need to increase the amount of people contacted or send them a slightly different message. There will always be minor adjustments that can be made to the program but the executions must remain ongoing forever or else you will see your customers defecting to other dealerships.

The number one source of new business—the person you are currently doing business with—is a concept that requires buy-in from dealership owners and managers in order to be successful. The math and logic sounds great and makes sense, but this business plan is a long commitment and necessitates a tireless execution that will require a great deal of effort and money. Over the last few years, some dealers and industry experts have jumped on the email-blast bandwagon and say there is no reason to send snail mail when you can send email. I couldn't disagree more, especially as the mailbox has become a wide open playing field with less mail being sent.

The reason you cannot depend on email alone is the open rates.

Open rates are low—currently somewhere around 20 percent if you check what NADA publishes. People who promote email make a good point, but I feel they are trying to step over dollars to make pennies. Go back to the equation of one percent of your customer base being in the market to buy in the next three to 10 days and think about whether you would rather have these buyers only get an email or get both an email and a letter in their mailbox. I like to explain the rationale of a dentist appointment to make better sense of it. Think about what you are most likely to remember and attend, a dentist appointment that you get an email about or a dentist appointment that you get a card in the mail as a reminder about. Then think about the dentist appointment that you received a phone call about after you got a card in the mail. I know which one I would remember and I also know that many people think of dentist and car dealerships in a similar light. Nobody really likes going to either one. But to get the service that you need, both are a necessary evil in your life.

A dealership that markets to its existing owners will generate traffic through sales and service to its owner body at a higher rate than if these customers are not contacted. These customers become a better source of revenue and are less apt to price shop on their next sale and service because they are familiar and comfortable with your place of business. While many dealerships use email and mail to contact their customers periodically throughout the year, I think personal contact is still the most untapped and underutilized area of business. The return on investment and dollars spent to keep an existing customer pale in comparison to the dollars needed to create a new customer. I can't stress enough that the number one source of new business is the person you are currently doing business with. I would invest my marketing dollars in this area before ever spending a penny talking to the masses.

3

THE CONTENTS OF A 30-SECOND COMMERCIAL

A lot of dealers and advertising agencies have no real grasp on how you make an effective 30-second retail car commercial. I see ads all the time in markets all across the country that are merely thrown together with little to no attention paid to the most important elements of the message. There are ads that have as many as five or six offers. Other ads run and never have a price or a compelling reason to buy. And you always see ads that make it impossible to tell which dealership the ad is for because the name only appears at the end. It is one of the most poorly executed areas of automotive marketing, and the real kicker is that it's the one that everybody sees! A lot of dealers and agencies have no written rules or firm structure on what does and doesn't need to be in their ads. Our creative and production departments are some of the things that have allowed our company to turn dealerships around quickly. Once we are hired, it's easy to out-promote the competition—especially when the competition is promoting with ineffective ads.

Every one of our ads has three things and three things only. We sell the event, price and who has it. You could also say that we are giving the viewer "a reason to buy, a reason to buy today and a reason to buy from us." It's just that simple. We are selling an event that's defined as "the reason why now is the time to buy and it is the best time to buy." Every month, every holiday, every manufacturer sale gives you a reason to have an event. There must always be a compelling reason to buy. Once you have the event, you must then have a price. There is no need to put a price on every model that you sell; the trick is to drive hot traffic to the hottest products. By the time the shopper has come down to the bottom of the purchase funnel, they have already made up their mind to buy. All we are doing is trying to make them buy from us. I believe wholeheartedly that in a tier three retail television spot, you can get away with not showing the car by focusing on the price alone. I use very little vehicle-running footage or pictures of cars during a TV spot. Everybody who is thinking about buying a Toyota Camry in the next three to 10 days already knows what it looks like, so why waste your dollars showing them the car again? The same is true with a Chevy Silverado. Every full-size truck intender already knows more about that truck than we can ever tell them in 30 seconds. So let's give them the reason to buy, reason to buy today and reason to buy from us.

Finally, the most important part of these three components is who has it. The store's name and logo must be prominent and mentioned at least four times in a 30-second spot. If you do this, then your name has been seen or heard every seven and a half seconds of the spot. This makes it nearly impossible for the viewer or listener to not know whose ad it is. You are committing one of the biggest crimes in creating a commercial if you have a finished 30-second spot and nobody can tell you who was being promoted. And not to mention the money spent by the dealer to promote it just went down the toilet.

I'm going to take you through the process of building an effective ad that will generate traffic and provide you with the necessary features every ad must have. Creating great commercials takes every bit as much firm process and technical detail as it takes being extremely talented and artistic. The technical detail comes from knowing an exact word count, having a set amount of time in every spot for the dealership's name and logo, knowing where the URL is going to go so that it makes a strong visual impact and having a set list of fonts and type styles that never change. The artistic aspects come from having a well-defined color pallet that meshes with the look of the manufacturer, a very effective and attention-getting opening, and using transitions to keep the viewer engaged instead of tuning your ad out. There must also be a great read from an announcer with a piece of music that matches the theme and tempo of the spot. It takes a combination of both technical detail and art to make a truly effective ad. When the two are combined, you have the ability to make a very memorable and favorable impression on the public. If a favorable impression has been made from an ad that delivers traffic to your door, then you have achieved success through automotive advertising.

To start the process you have to look at the technical side of the spot, starting with your word count. When I began my career in advertising I was told you could have 75 words in a 30-second spot. If you have ever written or attempted to write copy you may have heard a similar rule or might have just timed every spot with a stopwatch and never paid attention to word count. As the years went by and I watched more and more of our spots, I realized that they were too fast. They moved too fast and sounded too fast when I saw them on TV or heard them on the radio. With the help of our truly talented creative team of Dennis Johnson and Tori Reid, we redefined the rules by which we wrote copy. By the time the dust settled and we were happy with both the sound and speed of our ads, we were amazed to see that our best spots averaged 42 words in 30 seconds. This was absolutely shocking because for years we focused on not going past 75 words in a spot. By cutting the word count in half, we produced ads that garnered our dealers higher traffic counts and more awareness when dealers were measured for top-of-mind awareness through Nielson. Since making this surprising discovery, the ads we have produced have had far more impact and created a noticeable increase in traffic. I believe sticking to a spot with a lower word count will do far more to create traffic and increase awareness of a dealership than anything else.

Once you have settled on a precise word count, write copy that presents a reason to buy, a reason to buy today, and a reason to buy from *you*. Every spot should have no more than two prices on the two hottest products you have to sell. Do not fool yourself into thinking that you can run more than two offers in a 30-second spot and count on generating traffic. My preference is to focus on one vehicle with one offer in a spot, and then say the price four, maybe five times, which creates immediate recall and noticeable traffic for that vehicle. Generally the only time it is acceptable to have two vehicles with prices in the spot is if you have a smaller budget or are in a bigger market with less gross rating points. Focus on generating traffic using your hottest product(s) and let the traffic you bring in on those items help sell your cold merchandise. You cannot advertise your problems and create the kind of return needed. You must promote the best ones you have and they will take care of the rest.

The "reason to buy today" is always deemed "the event." There are literally hundreds of these. The ones that I have found to be the best are the ones that have two to three words in the name. The event names must always convey to the public that this is *the* time to buy and they always have to look big. If you think that your dealership will not be able to come up with new event names every month then I'll let you in on a little secret. All you need are 12! You can run a different month-long event every month and you can run them over and over for years and years to come. The public will forget about these almost immediately when they go off the air. So don't feel as if you are going to have to develop a new one every month for the rest of the time you are in business. The best events should be run over and over, as long as they are spread out and not run too often in the same year. An event in tier three advertising is no different than an event in tier one advertising. Your manufacturer most likely runs the same events over and over year after year. For example, Toyotathon, Honda Clearance, Nissan Bottom Line, Ford Truck Month, Chevy Red Tag and Hyundai Holidays are run every year. These events are just like your events only the contents inside the ad are different.

The final technical component is "who has it," also known as "the reason to buy from us." The dealership's name must be in the spot at least four times and you must always end the spot with a directional locator of how to physically find the store. One way to make the spot more recognizable is to personalize the merchandise that you are pricing. This may sound difficult but it is really very simple and here's how. If my name (John Paul) was the name of the dealership and I was merchandising a Toyota Camry at a particular price point, it would be said like this: "John Paul Toyota Camry $19,990." In these five words you just put the dealership name, name of the product, and the price together. This makes it impossible for the viewer or listener to not know whose Camry it is. Another way to maximize the dealership's name awareness is through the URL. Most all stores have a URL that matches their name with a dot-com on the end, and this should be said and shown often as a visual and audio element to further embellish the name of the dealership.

From a technical side, there is a list of items that should never be included in a tier three commercial. It's a laundry list, so here goes: miles per gallon and EPA ratings, safety ratings, resale value, third-party endorsements, local endorsements, manufacturers awards (unless it is one for largest volume), anything related to your service department, anything related to your parts department, mentions about your staff and any lines or copy points about how you do business. All of these items have no place in a spot designed to create new car traffic from your core products. Remember there are three tiers of automotive advertising and selling MPGs, crash test ratings, and resale value should be done at the tier one level. All of the points about your parts, service, people, and local awards should be told to the customers once they are on your lot. Don't try to tell them all of that to get them on your lot, as most people will not believe it or care about it. I like to use the phrase, "Tell them how great you are once you get them here." Many people are not going to believe a car dealership anyway due to the lack of trust and stigma that society has placed on our industry. If you get them in your dealership and you have a mantra of doing business the right way, then the customer will see it and the case is closed—you won! Keep these elements out of your spots because they really are not helping your sales.

Now you get to the artistic side of the process. This side evolves and changes every single day as the ever-changing opinions of the American public are swayed by what is seen on television and heard on the radio. The one thing our company has done to provide a consistent look without becoming stale creatively is through connectivity. Our dealerships are given certain elements that always remain the same even as the copy and event names change. The look of an ad can be consistent with what has been done in previous months and years. Incredible detail is paid to color pallets. For instance, where a Toyota dealer's ad will be dominated with reds, blacks, and grays, a Honda dealer's color pallet will be primarily blue, white and silver. This is done so that there is consistency throughout all our spots, but also so that there is connectivity back to that which ran in tier one and tier two ads for the manufacturer. Creating a consistent color pallet by brand is the first thing to be executed on the artistic side of the spot.

Once the color pallet is set, you must assemble the elements you will be using. You have an event name and some type of graphic, symbol or logo that will be shown to illustrate it. This will be your changing variable from spot to spot, but it must always be brilliant in color and bold in presentation. Remember: We have to make it look like the greatest buying event ever. The store logo and dealership name must be used early in the spot and you should work to find ways to keep it onscreen as long as possible in as many places as possible. The prices must always be big and should always be in colors that match your chosen pallet. Our company takes all of the guesswork out of font selection and type style by studying the most effective font choices and assigning them to a dealership. This means the font will never change unless given direction. This helps build the connectivity that we are working to create. If you are thinking that this sounds like we have taken the creativity out of being creative, you are wrong. By limiting the small decisions and factors that affect a spot like font selection, we allow ourselves more time to build incredible and believable themes. If you do the same thing, it will work the same way for your dealership and your marketing.

The announcer, tempo and music are what tie the spot together and give you the icing on the cake. As with other elements, we select a voice and delivery style for the dealership based on the type of market it is in and brand we are promoting. Some dealerships/brands are promoting louder and faster while others are more subtle and softer. This all depends on buyer demographics, what media has been selected and what the ultimate goal is for the dealership. A consistent voice and delivery style is just another element that builds consistency for a dealership. The music can fluctuate so it matches the style and speed of the event, but generally there needs to be a good deal of similarity in the sound. I have been asked the question over the years, "Should I just pick one piece of music and stick with it forever?" My answer is, "No." Different events and different ads will flow differently and thus you need flexibility with the music you want to use. (Not to mention that if you use the same music for years and years, the public may pay more attention to your music and less attention to the offers and events you are selling.) Music is memorable, but we are capturing connectivity through enough ways that you do not have to be painted in a corner and always use the same music.

In conclusion, for every one good tier three automotive ad I see there are 20 bad ones. Most dealers and advertising agencies have never been trained or formulated a cadence for what must be in each ad and what shouldn't. I have formulated the method laid out in this chapter over the last decade of creating ads and through the help of my father, Mike Strong, who has been creating automotive ads since the mid '70s. It can be a very simple process that is a lot of fun if you recognize that there is as much of a technical side as there is an artistic side. The result in traffic over time due to maintaining a focused message with a reason to buy, reason to buy today and reason to buy from us, can be astounding. The result in traffic over time from advertising one or two really hot products with a great offer can be amazing. The amount of additional gross profit that can be generated by this additional traffic will be tremendous. When you eliminate all the useless information that most people put into their ads, you have the ability to maximize your exposure and increase your product penetration. It is time to take a look at the manner in which your ads are built and refocus on the elements that are critical and you will be able to generate more traffic.

4

IT'S THAT TIME OF THE MONTH...EVERY MONTH

The one thing all great advertising plans and marketing strategies have in common is a well-laid-out monthly calendar. The calendar allows you to build your plan so you are able to maximize the best days and weeks of a month for increased traffic. Yes, you can drive traffic every single day of the year, but there is a reason that the car business is measured by the first 10 days, second 10 days, and last 10 days of a month.

What I have found in a lot of dealerships that are looking for help is that they fail to plan. Failing to plan has a direct correlation to failing to succeed. There is no way that an effective plan can be created by saying, "Well, what are we going to do next week?" A plan must be created and reviewed months in advance, and then looked at closely as you approach 30 days from its beginning. Dealerships that fail to plan and want to just "wing it" or do everything in the last hour never have a chance to build and sustain steady streams of traffic because there is no purpose to the plan. The plan is crafted by the deadline—having to do something quick and trying anything that comes along. The purpose of this chapter is to point out some of the most misused opportunities when it comes to planning out a calendar for all advertising executions.

The first thing that you have to do in developing a monthly plan is to review your store's sales history for the past 12 months. In looking at the last complete year, you are able to see which months generated the most sales and which generated the least. I have seen monthly sales volume vary all across the country. These variances can be a result of weather in Northern markets to increases in snowbird populations in Southern and Southwest markets. The start of football season can affect sales or a NASCAR event can shut down an entire city. The beginning or ending of a school year or even a thing as simple as the start or end of daylight savings time can affect your sales volume in a month. Breaking down a calendar to understand the critical timing of events and how these events have affected sales in the past gives you the opportunity to not make the same mistake twice. Start your calendar-building process by knowing what is happening (or has happened) in your market and how it affects your business.

Once you have a glimpse of the past 12 months in relation to sales volume, you can shift your focus to the future and planning out the next 12 months. Of critical importance is finding the months with five weekends in the coming year. By knowing the months that are going to have the most weekend selling days, you automatically know when your manufacturer objectives are going to be the highest. This is a telling sign: In these months, you must allocate more budget to cover more days and weeks of running media to generate traffic. The great thing about planning this out over 12 months is that you can map out which months to spend more and which months to spend less. Possibly the greatest thing about a five-weekend month is you actually get to cover three pay periods as opposed to only covering two in a four-weekend month.

Planning your promotions and media run dates around pay periods is nothing new. I didn't invent this principle, it has been around for decades but it is one I hear very few people talking about today. A lot of people still talk about running the last two or three weeks of a month, but very little attention is given to the dates in which most Americans get paid. Every calendar should have a footnote about which dates are the pay periods so this can be a place to look at creating additional traffic. Everyone still depends on money, especially to make big-ticket purchases. That's why focus is needed to plan and execute at a time when people have more disposable income to spend. There is more money for down payments, taxes, titles and buying of accessories when you target around monthly pay periods. Of course, not all people get paid twice a month. Some people are paid weekly, some once a month, some even once a year—but we are not looking at all the exceptions, we are looking at the masses. The mass population of America is paid twice a month and this should be at the very forefront of your planning.

As you take into consideration all these foundational elements of planning and actually begin selecting the days and weeks in which you are going to run your advertising, you must also look at how your store performs historically over the first 10 days, second 10 days, and last 10 days of a month. The majority of all stores start out slowly the first 10 days, then come on strong the closer they get to the end of the month. We all know why. It's a systemic part of the retail car business. Sales people and managers work less the first part of a month and then work themselves to the walls as the month comes to a close to try and "make their month." This is the time when your advertising should be running the most.

Again, we are living at the very bottom of the purchase funnel and talking to people who are planning to buy in the next three to 10 days. So this is when all your forms of media and owner body contact should occur. I have seen some stores that can promote early in the month and generate traffic that equals sales, but the entire dealership must be prepared to handle this traffic and this type of execution.

The typical dealership runs its heaviest advertising from days 10 through 25 of the month in order to build momentum for a strong month-end close. This allows you to capitalize on the mid-month pay period, and by the time you get to the end-of-the-month pay period you have had a heavy presence for the last two weeks. With the right message, reach and frequency you can put yourself in the right place to talk to the largest number of buyers in the market. Through the years, our industry as well as many others, has conditioned both itself and its buyers that this is the best time to buy big-ticket items. Whether this is right or wrong, this is the way it is. When you accept and work to this strength you put yourself in a position to be highly successful. Knowing how to plan and execute a month based on these elements allows you to create a plan that is going to generate more traffic than if you pay no attention to buying cycles and shopping patterns and just run your advertising blindly.

Now that the basics are in place, it is time to get crafty. This is my favorite part because it is where you separate the men from the boys and the pros from the amateurs. Now is when you look for the hidden opportunity. In the last three years I have only heard one other person in the automotive industry talk about planning an event around a full moon. (The person I am referring to shall remain anonymous, but he/she runs the largest volume dealership of their make in the entire country.) There is a reason that hospital emergency rooms are more crowded on days in which there is a full moon. People tend to act a little crazier and make more impulse decisions when we are in a full moon period. Most dealers or agencies have never paid attention to the lunar cycles or even studied the Farmer's Almanac to predict weather patterns when planning their advertising. This is why I stated that we are separating the men from the boys. Planning an event around full moons has generated so much traffic for our dealers over the years that every calendar that is planned by our company notes the full moon dates each month. Sometimes a full moon falls on a day that isn't worth promoting, like the first Tuesday of a month, but other times it may fall on a Friday that also happens to be a mid-month pay period. When it falls on the latter, that is a day that warrants a big-time event.

This is not a commandment to go out and run a moonlight madness sale one weekend out of every month. It's a challenge to go out and find any and every extra opportunity in a month that can generate incremental traffic for your store. The event you run during a full moon doesn't even have to be a moonlight madness sales event; it can be completely different. We are not trying to use a one-size-fits-all creative approach. A red tag sale will also generate traffic. The purpose here is to look at the calendar and find hidden opportunities because they're in every month.

If you were to run a moonlight madness sale though, when do you think it is craftier to run one? On a day when you have a new moon or can hardly see the moon? Or on a day when you have a full moon that dominates the nighttime sky and consumers' shopping patterns have proven they are more likely to make impulse decisions? Your call—but I think you see my point.

Another element that has been around for years, yet seems most dealers and agencies have forgotten, is a hard-hitting one day sale. Unless you have lived under a rock for the past decade you have probably seen the one day sale once a quarter from Macy's, one of the largest and most successful retail department stores. For a dealership, the one day sale is a chance to create excitement both with the public as well as within your staff. A well-planned one day sale can turn a Monday into a Saturday for you based on the traffic it can create and the sales you can pick up. A one day sale can be any day of the week. There are no rules as long as you build the hype around the fact that the deals are only going to be this good for one day.

Oftentimes when planning and picking out the best time for a one day sale, I look to any Monday holidays or government/school/banking holidays. Below is a listing of ones to start with.

- Martin Luther King, Jr. Day
- Presidents' Day

- St. Patrick's Day (better start it early though)
- Memorial Day
- July 5th
- Labor Day
- Columbus Day
- Veterans Day
- Black Friday

Again, these are not the only times of the year you can run a one day sale, but these are days when most businesses are closed, kids are out of school and government employees have time off. These days should all be studied and reviewed in your marketing plan just like Saturdays because you can generate an incredible amount of traffic for an average weekday.

Also, look to normal days of the week where you have the opportunity to capitalize. If the month ends on a Wednesday, then there is no reason not to have a one day sale on the Tuesday before. If you have a five-weekend month, then nothing says that the first Friday of the month could not be used as a one day sale. If your entire sales staff works on a Thursday, then pick one Thursday a month and run the sale. There are many reasons to run one. The only things that keep people from them are usually a lack of budget or a management team that has a hard time motivating its people to do anything outside of the box. I understand that people get in a rhythm and that things like this generally are looked at as incurring more marketing costs, but the costs pale in comparison to the traffic and gross that can be generated from them.

Many things must be studied to effectively plan a month to make your advertising dollars generate the maximum amount of traffic. First look at how that month performed in the past and if there were any interruptions, whether seasonal or market specific that would inhibit your ability to generate traffic in this month. It is best to plan out an entire calendar year at once and then go back to revisit each month about 30 days before advertising starts so that you can look for anything you might have missed. When planning the days and weeks that you run your media, be sure to remember the "first 10 days, second 10 days, and last 10 days of the month" rule and be sure your calendar is set accordingly. Unless your dealership shows incredible success each month from beginning to end, you will see more traffic if you stick to running your media somewhere between the 10th and 25th day of a month. Take this plan and run it this way every month, which allows you to build consistency. Don't try to recreate your plan just because a page in the calendar turns over. This plan should be consistent and executed month in and month out.

Finally, separate yourself from the other guys and put forth the extra effort in finding all the hidden opportunities. Look for full moons, five-weekend months, pay periods and the best days to run a one day sale. It's the difference between a good traffic count and a great traffic count. This opportunity will not be knocking on your door. You are going to have to find it by looking to leverage every opportunity that you can find, and then be creative with it. By doing all of the above, you will generate more traffic on a month-in and month-out basis for your dealership.

5

PRICE SELLS CARS

The single most effective way to generate new car traffic in a dealership is to advertise the price. Price comes in the form of the advertised selling price or what the monthly payment would be based on the term of the loan. I know of no other way to state this other than to simply say, "Price sells cars." The very foundation of this stems from the retail automotive purchase funnel featured in Chapter One. By the time people move from brand awareness to product consideration and all the way down the funnel to purchase intent, the buyer has made up their mind what they are going to buy. Now all they need to decide is who to buy it from.

When the customer has settled on the exact model car and even specific colors, all that's left is to decide where to shop based on who they perceive to have the best deal. The three types of traffic tell us that we will have natural, owner body and created traffic. So all shoppers will fall into one of these categories. Even if the shoppers are your own "natural" or "previous owners," you still must promote a strong price presence to remind people why they should do business with you. The customer may not remember why they bought from you before, and every manufacturer has a research study and data about what percentage of their customers are loyal to the dealer that sold them last time. I take very little of that information seriously because when people enter the buying cycle, a large percentage of them are looking for the best price first and foremost. Some people will shop from a company they have done business with before because of a sense of trust or an existing relationship even if that means they pay a little more. But if there is too great of a difference in price they may not buy from you. An organization with a long-tenured, low-turn-over sales staff may be able to convert more previous customers even at a higher advertised price, but this is pretty rare and should be treated as the exception, not the rule.

Some previous customers may have a preferred person at a dealership that they are more comfortable buying from, even if they know they are paying a little more. Some buyers will pay a premium for ease and a sense of security. But this is not how you are going to form and cultivate your "created traffic" because they have no preexisting reason that they should buy from you. Do not misunderstand—it is a dream come true for any automotive dealership to have customers with this type of loyalty and sentiment, but it is incredibly rare. If your people work that well with customers, imagine what they could do if you covered them up every day with new traffic that you created via your promotions and advertising!

The purpose of new car advertising can be broken down into two simple points:

1. Stay on the mind of your "natural traffic" and "owner body traffic." These are people that should be shopping with you automatically and thinking of you first when they re-enter the buying cycle. Your message and perception of having an incredibly low price and always having a reason to buy will reinforce that "they got a great deal" and that you must be a great place to do business. (This goes back to the "safety in numbers" premise – they continue to feel good about their

decision to buy from you because your dealership is full of other shoppers.)

2. Position your dealership in the marketplace to gain exposure among those that would not otherwise shop your store. "Created traffic" is the essence of selling more vehicles, growing profits and market share among the general public. When people in the market see a dealership promoting incredible prices and reasons to buy today, they will consider you even if you are not on their primary shopping list because of the fear of losing out on a good deal.

Understanding that your new car advertising should be broken down into these main points will help you understand the necessity of advertising the price as your main proposition in your ads. When you condition yourself that this is how the public buys the decision to build an aggressive price-promoting message is very simple to make.

To form a parallel to other industries, think of large appliance and furniture retailers that you have seen aggressively promoting for decades. They do not say things like, "Come see us. We're great people," or "We have great products, just come see the prices when you get here!" The one thing they all have in common is they always promote a hot product at a great price. Think of Sears, Best Buy, Macy's, The Home Depot or Lowe's. All of these companies are promoting a particular sales event followed up with multiple price points to generate traffic. A dealership should be no different in its thinking or planning. The price is what all big-ticket-item buyers are looking for, and it is what generates traffic to stores the day the ads hit the air or run online. What I spend a great deal of my time discussing and reminding dealerships is that they are a retailer. They have to think like a retailer, act like a retailer and promote like a retailer. That is why all the companies mentioned above have been so successful. They have created an awareness and perception over time that lives in the minds of the American public.

At this point perception becomes reality. The dealership that has top-of-mind awareness due to years and years of advertising and promoting price is going to at least have a shot of being shopped by the customer who is in the market to buy. Whether the consumer has done business with you before or lives in close proximity or miles away, you have created an image that you have a desired product at a great price. Once you create the image, you have to run it over and over, week after week and month after month to pound that message into the mind of the buyer. The consistency will build up your dealership so that they think you advertise so much that you obviously must do a lot of business. When they see this it drives home the "safety in numbers" theory because people like to do business where business is being done. Nobody wants to go to a dealership and see him or herself as the only person on the lot. If they pay attention and see there are no other customers or shoppers there, they will question your methods and practices which may cause them not to buy. Think of this as being back in school and how the first day would be dreaded. You always had some jitters about starting a new year, but the minute you hit the door of the school and saw people you knew having to go through the same thing it always got a little easier.

Now that there is a clear understanding of what price is and how much the retail buying process is affected by price alone, it is time to talk about how you offer price. Price takes the form of total price to buy and the monthly payment over the term of the loan to purchase. The reason that these two forms are so paramount is that when buyers are researching and shopping for vehicles, both online or on the lot, every vehicle has an MSRP on the window and every vehicle has a price posted online. (Every vehicle should have a price posted online unless you are selling cars on Mars.) The reason that a straight-up price takes such importance is because when people are at the bottom of the buying cycle, they already have an idea of what the vehicle costs. They have to have a good idea of this otherwise there would be no way they could know if they can afford it or not. People are looking for a price because that is how they know what they can afford and whether or not they can be stepped up or down when looking at trim levels and accessories.

Payments also come into play when talking directly to the buyer in terms of how much they can afford per month in their budget. Some brands perform better with payments than others, especially as you get into high-line and luxury brands. Not to say that volume brands don't do well with payments, but most volume brands have base model cars that can be advertised with a price somewhere between $10,000 and $40,000. This just notes that due to higher price and higher value of the vehicles most luxury brands can be more easily put into terms if a payment is promoted. When people are able to see how much they pay per month it can be the tipping point that finally pushes them over the edge and brings them down from consideration to purchase intent in the funnel.

There is a lot of debate and discussion about payments—whether to advertise a purchase payment or a lease payment in your message. I think the answer and long-term solution of this can be decided very simply: If you are in a geographical area of the country that performs well or above average with leases, then you can center your payment message on leasing. However, if you are in an area where leases are not as well received or your dealership does not have high-lease penetration, then you have to take a serious look at whether leasing is going to generate traffic for you.

If the buyers in your market, as well as dealership sales and management personnel, know the value of leasing and have been conditioned to be more adapt to lease, then you can promote it as your price premise. It is an absolute necessity to make sure your employees are trained on selling leasing and the ability to paint the value picture of why they should lease. If leasing is going to be your main price premise you have got to make sure it can be handled to perfection.

If your market doesn't have high-lease penetration, you may be trying to push a market that cannot be moved with tier three advertising dollars. Trying to change the mindset of how people buy can be nearly impossible to do and will take an enormous amount of time and money. In most cases if the market is not a market with a high propensity to lease, don't even try it. Even if your brand is one that has a high-lease penetration, you are not going to be able to move customers using a different way to buy.

In the last couple years more and more volume brands have recharged their dealers on leasing and lease training within the stores. There is no doubt that having a customer who is going to be forced to either buy a vehicle outright or turn it in within 24 to 48 months of the lease signing is an advantage to the dealership in terms of repeat business. The only thing that must be watched—and watched closely—is if your brand has a strong enough lease presence as well as your market, otherwise you will be forced to stick to price and or purchase payment.

Advertising purchase payments have been incredibly downplayed in the last 20 years because of the rise of leasing. When leasing became popular and manufacturers began running a lot of leases at the tier one and tier two levels, many dealers simply quit using purchase payments as a primary means to sell a price premise. I think it happens to be a great method and one that can get a lot of people to consider you or your product if properly promoted. Many dealerships still mark these payments on windshield tags or paint them directly on the windshield of cars on the lot for shoppers to see, but very few run them in their media or online advertising. It is an effective way to promote payments if you are in a market or area that does not lease and it is a great way to hold gross or attract secondary/special finance buyers.

Regardless of whether you advertise a price or payment, the bottom line is that your message will be more effective if it has one or the other. Running an advertisement for a tier three dealership without a price will help drive up your awareness, but traffic is not created on awareness alone. Traffic is created from awareness *and* an effective offer. Traffic is created by causing fear of loss in the mind of the buyer: If they do not at least give you a chance, they may be missing out. Traffic is created by consistently advertising a compelling reason to buy and reason to buy today. Remember that you are only talking to one percent of the market that is in the market to buy in the next three to 10 days and everyone else who sees your ad just sees a message. The power of the "price sells cars" premise is based on consistently running incredible prices, making it a compelling reason to buy. That is how you elevate your dealership in the market and make people scared not to shop with you before they buy.

There are dealerships out there that have never run a price (and probably never will) that are effective. Remember this is the exception and not the rule. To increase traffic which in turn will increase sales and market share, price is hands down the way to go. It must be advertised and remain consistent month after month and year after year in order to accomplish what has been mentioned.

In order to remain consistent with your price premise, this is a decision that must be made and managed by the owner, dealer or general manager. The reason for the structure and ultimate management is it cannot be changed or altered based on market or inventory conditions. If it is changed without warrant and not properly ready to execute month after month, it will fail. If pricing and development of the price/payment strategy is left up to anyone else other than the person in charge, it stands to be broken and will not accomplish what is needed.

My opinion of this comes from many years of seeing great programs put into place only to watch them fail when someone other than the top decision maker is involved. The person who is ultimately in charge of setting the total dealership advertising budget and approving the plan is the one who should remain responsible for making sure the price strategy stays in place. A lot of people in top management will tend to approve and oversee the total advertising picture yet want to hand off the pricing and payment elements to someone beneath them. This can be death to your program. If you are in charge of advertising and know what the full plan for the dealership is, you have to pay attention and be in charge of this strategy all the way through. It is the only way to insure that you stay consistent with your price message; the only way to insure your people are being trained how to handle the traffic; the only way to make sure your inventory manager is ordering your cars based on the plan in place. And most importantly, the only way you can make sure your people, including your advertisers, are accountable for the results and return on investment that is gained.

In conclusion, I have worked hands-on with literally hundreds of dealerships and all major brands on their marketing strategies and advertising plans. I have seen good markets, bad markets and even what we have come to call "heart-attack markets." While some plans have worked better than others and some plans have failed before they were ever out of the gate, there is one statement that is the very core of retail automotive advertising: "PRICE SELLS CARS!"

Price hits at the very essence of the way American consumers buy big-ticket items. It is all they know. It's the way they have been conditioned to shop. This carries across all facets of media from the Internet to the television to the mailbox. Whatever your message is and whomever it is sent to, you will be more effective and deliver a greater return on investment, along with more traffic to your front door, when price dominates.

More dealerships have been turned around, elevated and built into giants in their markets by an intense effort and totally focused plan based on advertising the vehicle price. Remember, price comes in the form of the total amount for the vehicle as well as the monthly payment, but having price at the very heart of your message is the most critical piece of the puzzle in today's climate.

6

CASH CARS ARE CONSTANT AND RETAIL FIRST RULES

Over the last decade, it has been very interesting to watch the trends that used car buyers and franchise dealers have gone through. It always seems that there is a flavor of the month or a favorite among dealers and managers when it comes to which vehicles to stock and how to go about finding these vehicles. Through the changes in the economy and peaks and valleys of used car popularity, I have developed one common denominator that can create traffic no matter where you are or what kind of dealership you have: Cash cars are a constant source of steady used car sales, and if you create a retail-first mind-set in your dealership through the reconditioning process, this can be highly profitable for you on a regular basis. Or, if that is too much to remember, try this: "If it rolls, then roll it!"

The biggest jaw-dropping thing that I witness is a used car manager or buyer who walks into the dealer or owner's office and says,

"I am going to auction to buy a truckload of _____ because they are hot and I know we can sell them quickly." Too many times the person in charge who is putting their money behind this investment will nod their head in agreement without any questioning or discussion. This is like buying stocks from a broker who cold-calls you and says they have a great stock tip that they know will make you money, "So go ahead and give me $100,000 today before it's too late." Even if you knew the person you still wouldn't do this without the slightest bit of research, would you?

Very few dealerships research and study historical data regarding which makes and models sell on their lot. They should consider the time of year, price points and length of time they kept these cars in inventory before they were sold. The sad thing is, the tools are out there to do this and have been for a couple of years, but too many times used car inventory management is based on "I think" and "we should try this" mentalities, which is a terrible way to spend your inventory dollars. No longer does a dealership have to guess at what they should buy or what moves best in the store. The technology is ready for you. The question is, are you ready for it?

More often than not, the answer to this question is no. Stores and managers are not ready to change their inventory and stocking practices. People in the stores are not regimented enough to use these tools on a consistent basis as needed and a good tool often goes to waste. Now, not every dealership is this way; some have embraced used car inventory software such as V-Auto and First Look, but the stores who actually do this right are few and far between. I have no vested interest in either of these companies. I've never been paid to endorse them or recommend them in any manner – but I see their capabilities, and compared to the alternative (which is nothing), they are the only game in town.

As a promoter, you are only going to be effective with generating traffic when that traffic finds something they want to buy either on the lot or online. This is why I urge dealers to use some type of source for stocking used car inventory. If you are watching trends and looking out for potential issues, you will be more consistent and more profitable than you otherwise would be as a used car operation and you will be able to create a more consistent advertising message around your used car inventory. The best promotions are those that drive people to you to buy exactly what you sell.

The trend that I see constantly is the emergence of less expensive "cash cars" on lots of new car franchise dealers. Yes, independents and smaller operations buy here as well. Pay-here stores have carried these cars for years, but now new car dealers are getting in the game because this source of business has become low-hanging fruit. It provides a great source of revenue to multiple departments in the dealership, including service and parts. There is more demand in present day for these vehicles than I have ever seen.

Think back to the events of September 2008, and everything that has happened since regarding "The Great Recession." As housing values and personal wealth among Americans dropped like a rock over recent years, people have had to adjust their mode and preference of transportation. To sum it all up, a lot of people don't have the ability to buy the kind of car they did five or 10 years ago. This has increased the need for cash cars and the reasons why they should always be part of your inventory, merchandising and advertising mix.

These vehicles are also one of the best sources for creating "organic traffic" to your store or website because of how many people are constantly looking for them. Consider it free advertising. You are going to pull people in who never would have shopped you otherwise, who either drive by and see the cars or find them online. Sure, you may have a little cost to place them online on something like Craigslist, eBay or AutoTrader, but that cost will pale in comparison to other advertising dollars that you will spend. The secret is to stock them and make them visible. Showcase these cars where people can see them, both online as well as on the physical lot. If you hide them or make it so that people cannot see them, you are not doing yourself any justice.

Merchandising these vehicles is the next step to take after you have made them visible to shoppers. Show pricing, features, details and anything else that you would do on the other pre-owned vehicles you carry. Give each of these cars accurate descriptions on the website and your online listings. Remember that every used car has a different story to tell—so tell it. Just because they cost less doesn't mean you should merchandise them less. They should be detailed and cleaned like all your other vehicles. Use window stickers, hang tags, was/is pricing and price reductions to show that these vehicles are bargains and warrant the shopper's attention. If people cannot see the information they will not know the information, so make it easy to find.

Many dealers who do this effectively on their websites have an entirely different section for these vehicles, naming them "The Bargain Row" or "Under $10k Cars." Some even go as far to call them "Cash Cars." The names will vary from store to store but the concept is the same. Display and merchandise these vehicles on the two platforms that you get the majority of your used car traffic from: your physical lot and your website.

I have worked with dealers who do everything from creating special sections of the lot or rented tents, to even parking some of the cars on tractor trailers to make it seem like they are going to auction. One of my favorite executions was when a dealer and I wrapped the side of a 24-foot delivery truck that he had taken in on trade to advertise our "Used Cars Under $5,995" theme. If you can dream it or scheme, it then you can do it. This merchandising will be one of the least expensive forms of advertising you do, and will still manage to turn these vehicles through your inventory on a quick basis.

Once you have found and merchandised the inventory it is time to advertise it. It still amazes me how many people outside the automobile industry do not grasp the concept that new car franchise dealers also sell used cars. I hear it constantly from people who are far removed from the world of automotive advertising and retailing who just "never thought about a Toyota dealer selling used cars." While this may seem hard to fathom in the current age of digital information, some people never think about it in these terms. Remember, the majority of the public only thinks about cars when they are in the purchase funnel to buy one. Look at what CarMax has done and how successful they have become. The mass public only knows them as a used car dealership (and a big one at that).

If you want to get the message out about these cars, think in terms of the way that you advertise your new cars. If you buy television, cable, digital, radio, mail or even newspaper—these cash cars need to be promoted in the same way. With your new car advertising you have most likely found what you feel is the most effective form of media to reach your local market and immediate backyard. Use this media the same way that you would for used cars. Obviously these cars are a natural fit to be promoted online because many people looking to buy used cars start there, but do not be afraid to drive some real media weight and dollars behind these cars.

When you are advertising for these cars you must also think in terms of a special credit message. These cars are like a magnet for the credit challenged, so your message and your media need to adhere to this demographic as well. Some stores are not able or equipped to handle special finance and that's fine, but these cars will attract some of the credit criminals who are looking for something very cheap to drive. In no way does stocking these pieces make you a special credit store, but if you are one then your possibilities are endless.

The time of the month is another vital factor that dealers need to consider regarding cash cars (and used cars in general for that matter). There are no manufacturer incentives, rebate programs, or sales objectives tied to these cars. This means you don't have to wait for any specific information to advertise them. My advice to dealers who want to promote cash cars is to start very early in the month. These are great ads to run the first seven to 10 days of a month while all other dealers and regional new car advertisers are waiting to get new commercials produced with new programs that were announced the first of the month. Hit it hard and hit it early, and you can build momentum faster in a month than you ever dreamed.

After getting an early start in promoting, stick to your paydays and month ends. In most cases, the buyers for these cars will be dependent on the next paycheck for all or part of the payment they are going to have to make. It never hurts to promote these cars at the same time you promote your new cars either. There are always buyers in the market for these vehicles. Just because you are advertising new or regular pre-owned doesn't mean you cannot sell these as well.

The final piece to the puzzle involves everyone in the dealership understanding that "retail first" rules. I have watched firsthand in hundreds of dealerships where the new car department, used car department and service department do not see eye to eye on the reconditioning of used cars. The main culprit usually has something to do with everyone being paid based on what their department does—and having a little bit of ego at stake. The new car department wants to create volume and gross, looking good for all their peers in the industry, while the used car department generally wants to hold good grosses, have little customer heat and get great rates on reconditioning from the shop. Oh yeah, used car guys generally want their cars made front-line ready first before any customer cars are run through service. Then you have the service guys who want to have costly parts and labor charges added for all the cars they recondition and don't want somebody from used cars telling them to hurry up.

If this sounds all too familiar and you don't think you can train and compensate all teams to work together, then do not even try. This is like a paradigm change for most dealerships but one that must happen or everything else mentioned about these cars goes up in smoke. There must be a commitment from all three departments for a "retail first" mindset. A lot of the cars that will end up as your cash cars are not going to come from auctions. (I see about 75 percent come in from trades.) This means it's all up to you to organize the team and maximize the inventory opportunity within the four walls of your dealership.

Cash cars are king, and so is cash for managers. So with this commitment must come compensation—but you probably already knew that. Take control of your own destiny by retailing lower-end used cars and you will witness the creation of more incremental traffic to your dealership than you thought possible. There are several steps to making this work, but there are far more rewards in the end.

7

THE FOUR A'S FOR HOLIDAY MONTHS

When thinking about holiday months and what a huge impact they have on retail car shopping, I am reminded of a gem once offered to me by a dealer with over 40 successful years in the business. "If you consistently bank on a holiday weekend to save your month, you're making a solid investment in losing your ass." No dealership can survive by waiting or hoping to do all their business in one weekend to save a month. I don't care if you run one of the largest volume dealerships in the world, holding out for the holidays to make your month can lead to colossal failure.

The secret to holiday-month success is a steady and consistent flow of traffic. The key is making sure you have a plan that creates success early and often in the month so you can build momentum from day one. While the holidays fall at different times of the month during the peak season, all too often your internal staff will be waiting for the "traffic bus" to show up during a day or weekend that is big in their minds because it is a holiday. The only problem with this mindset is what happens when the bus doesn't show up and you do not have the type of holiday sale that you had planned on. With that in mind, I have developed what I call the "Four A's" for making holiday months strong from start to finish.

ACCELERATE

Make sure your advertising frequency starts the month at a strong level and then accelerates to reach its peak moving into the holiday weekend. Momentum is the key. If you consistently hammer your message home prior to a holiday-weekend event, you've already established top-of-mind awareness and solid traffic for your dealership. By starting to advertise early, you have the ability to pull more people into the market to buy your product.

Sometimes you have to change your thinking in order to accomplish this accelerated pace. I have talked to dealers for years about running earlier in months like May and December and not waiting for the last five days of the month to "take care of them." There is no substitute for getting a smoking start out of the gate and getting your sales pace up before you ever get to the holiday. I have often seen stores that generate more gross and create more opportunities for themselves because they have such a substantial lead.

You also have to take into account that on the actual holiday itself, traffic may be light because people are taking the day to travel, see family, or simply not have to deal with the hassle of buying a car. This doesn't mean the whole weekend or days leading up to the holiday will be slow – just do not be surprised if every holiday is not as big as it once was for you.

ACCLIMATE

If your market trends toward out-of-town activities during holiday weekends, consider holding a pre-holiday sales event and offering discounts and savings early so that shoppers can take advantage while they are in town. It's a good traffic-producing strategy even for stores that traditionally have a heavy turnout for holiday weekends. People have always said the early bird gets the worm, so offering an early-bird special is a great opportunity to build traffic.

When holding a presale, one very effective tool to use is targeted direct mail, email or outbound calling. For one, people have not yet left town and are accessible to a specifically targeted offer. When there is a tangible or physical offer in someone's hands, it can create more urgency in their mind, especially if there is a deadline in the form of an upcoming holiday that could delay the purchase. All forms of media can be effective but when looking to jump the gun on a holiday weekend, it is always a wise move to consider some form of direct contact to reach your audience.

Urgency is the key. Make sure that your message has a very specific deadline and that nobody is confused about when the offer ends. There will be no residual effect of your sales event when someone returns from a holiday or out-of-town trip, so it is crucial to make sure that the days are called out and media is bought vertically in order to drive traffic prior to this date. Being aggressive and urgent are the two keys to success in holding a pre-holiday sale.

ACCENTUATE

Historically, May, March, July, August and December are five of the strongest retail car-buying months of the year, so don't hold anything back. Present your strongest offers across all mediums in the boldest and most attention-getting ways. Have people and merchandise "ready and steady" so that you do not run out of the core products and do not run your people to the ragged edge. It does no good if you plan a grand sales event and run out of your best-selling products in the best colors the first or second day. This type of planning generally has to be done 60 to 90 days in advance to insure you have the right inventory.

Make your sales event "larger than life." The way to put your dealership ahead of all others is to make your sale look, feel and sound bigger than what anyone else is doing. This is not to say you must spend more money than everybody else, but accentuating a sale can be done in large part through your creative. The creative needs to sell the sizzle and carry this sizzle across as many forms of media as you can so that you can increase the audience reach. I always refer back to the old line "activity breeds activity," and if your sale looks and sounds like it has people knocking the doors down to come in, they typically will.

ACTIVATE

You can't win the championship if your team is sitting on the sideline. Activate your staff by holding sales meetings, a kickoff breakfast, the promise of a post-sale thank-you dinner or anything else you can think of. Also monetary spiffs never hurt any sales force, especially when you remember that "cash is king." Get balloons, posters, banners or whatever elements can be stuck to the showroom walls, hung from the ceilings or draped across the front of the dealership. The goal is to scream to the public that you are having a sale. In terms of "activating a sale," there is no end to how far you can go. We have used everything from giant inflatable dinosaurs, hot-air balloons, celebrities, skywriters…just about everything that can be thought of to create and sustain the hype. This also serves as a constant reminder to your people that the "sale is on," and a lot of times that can help motivation just as much as anything.

Remember, having a sale is doing nothing more than taking the common and making it uncommon. Your team must be engaged from start to finish in making the sale a success and capturing the momentum that you want in order to make it a great month. The holiday months can and should be the most successful and profitable months of the year for your business.

The four major holiday months, May, July, August and December are the months that can either make your year incredible or mediocre. These are the months we strive for as automotive retailers and marketers. There will be months where there are large factory incentives, vehicle closeouts and other factors that create success, but making the most of these holiday months can take your business and your profits to the next level, so make them count. Be engaged in all facets of your operation and with the right amount of traffic, you will not be disappointed.

8

HOT TRAFFIC SOLVES COLD MERCHANDISE

When the month of August rolls around, year after year, it's the same thing with auto dealers. As they are selling their way through higher-volume summer months, inventory from manufacturers starts to get a little scarce. The focus on which vehicles are going to be advertised can start to change. Regardless if the market is good or bad, most dealers sell their way through their most popular products. By the end of August they can be in a situation where they have to choose which vehicles are going to be their marketing weapons in September and October. In most situations, unless a new model is being launched or production cycles have been altered, this time of the year is when the industry sees itself in "sell down" mode. It has been called everything from model year-end clearance, closeout, sell down, out with the old/in with the new, and the list goes on.

There is one major trap that some dealers and marketers get caught in during this time. They tend to start advertising their problems. You can name a lot of problems that can affect a dealership in all kinds of different ways, but a major problem with any store, regardless of the make or location, is aged new car inventory. When it comes to aged inventory, it doesn't matter how good a dealer you are or how good your ordering practices are, it is something that is going to bite you if you are in this business. Whether you plan your floor plan or have another source for financing, letting your new car inventory get old is something that negatively affects the profitability of every dealership.

Aged inventory can be a primary result of two things. First, the vehicle you have was ordered in the wrong color or has the wrong content, and second, the vehicle is a model line that has gotten cold or was never hot from the start. Regardless of how you get there, every dealership has aged inventory, and the only way to get through it is to sell your way out of the situation. The manufacturer may or may not be able to help you with incentive money and rebates on these cars. In fact, you can bet if you are the only one with the aged inventory, they aren't going to help you with it. However, if they have the same problem with the same inventory then help is on the way.

Aged inventory greatly affects the profit of the new car sales department. Most dealers holding these vehicles for a longer than average time in inventory will either sell them at a loss to just get rid of them or pay their sales force such high cash incentives that it leaves zero gross in the deal. Not to mention the fact that this aged vehicle is taking up space that could be given to a more popular model that is going to turn faster and generate more profit for the store. Every automaker has them and nobody is exempt from having at least a couple of products that are not popular or high-volume units. The problem that I see too many dealers do at this time of year is focus on the merchandise problem rather than paying attention to what is selling the best. Too much effort is put on these cars from the space they take up on your lot and website, to how much of your advertising budget is spent to generate traffic on them. Just think for a second about the money that the manufacturer spends at the tier one level and regional advertising spends at the tier two level. If these messages cannot move this car then there is no way a dealer at the tier three level with limited funds can ever expect to move this unit. You are simply going to have to go after the traffic for this vehicle or model in another way.

THE TWO WAYS TO SOLVE COLD MERCHANDISE

1. Take the specific vehicle or the model line and make an offer that sounds too good to be true. Make this be so amazing and such an opportunity that people will at least give these cars a look. The following are real examples that have worked over the years:

The Pontiac Sunfire Sellathon

This happened in August 2004, when General Motors made the illustrious Pontiac Sunfire. Our dealer had over-ordered that year and done a horrible job at selling them throughout the year. This was a volume dealership so the Sunfires had piled up quickly on us. We looked up one day and saw there were 125 of them in inventory. They were selling an average of six a month so you can imagine how big of an issue this car was going to be, especially considering the fact that the model line was being discontinued and there would not be any more made. So we came up with the "Sunfire Sellathon" and advertised that we had 75 Pontiac Sunfires all priced at $12,995 and 50 more at similar prices. With the current incentives we had, this was about the best price you could find and made it easy for customers to decide not *if* they wanted a Sunfire, but *which one* they wanted. All cars were priced the same. Lucky for us this was a very large military market and, at the time, Pontiac was still a decent brand. With this price point, it was a very good entry-level car for this market. We ran this message for 30 days, saw some immediate traction, and went from selling six in a month to 30. Still with over 90 left in inventory, we came back the following month and ran a countdown. Our message was, "So many people came to buy the amazing $12,995 Sunfire last month we decided to repeat it."

So that month, we again continued to sell our way down through these Sunfires until we reached the last week of the year with a final message that said, "This is the last time you can ever buy a Sunfire and the only ones left are all priced at $12,995." We ended up having to take some major losses on those last units, but we had taken on a product that was as cold as ice and in just four months went from only selling an average of six per month to selling 30 per month. It also helped the dealer get out of a potentially awful financial situation.

The Special Shipment of Escalades

This example happened early in the summer. A dealer had more Escalades eating his floor plan up than he knew what to do with. Obviously there are not heavy rebates on these and it is hard to find an attractive lease payment on a vehicle that is $60,000 or more. So we went about this problem in a different way. Escalades were slow everywhere, even at the auctions, and values were dropping. So the dealer bought a dozen pre-owned Escalades way back-of-book value for current-year model vehicles. We themed the sale around, "We just received a special shipment of Escalades that are now 40% off original MSRP." These were used vehicles, but the same model year of the aged inventory. There was nothing deceptive about the ad. We never called them new. We even said that these vehicles had been shipped direct to us from a regional auction, and disclaimed that they were used vehicles in the television ad and online. We had vehicles tagged and signs made on the lot that showed particular Escalades at $20k less than the original MSRP.

What happened next was magical. We attracted all kinds of people. Some were luxury buyers and some were not, but the traffic counts literally increased tenfold. True luxury buyers came to see if this was real or a gimmick and they found that it was real and the Escalades were all parked on the lot and tagged. The next part is possibly the best of all. While most dealerships separate new cars from used cars on their lot, for this sale this dealer combined all new and used inventory together, parking all Escalades alongside each other. That probably was the best part about the execution of this sale and why it worked so well so fast. People chose their Escalade based on color, price and options rather than model year. This approach helped to get the dealer out of a bad situation. I will admit that I have never seen a dealer sell this many Escalades—ever. I haven't seen many dealers who will go out and invest further in a slow product line to help move that product line quicker. But if done right it will work.

Pay Once…Drive for Two

While Toyota has done almost everything right, the Scion brand may still be in question. This dealer looked up one day and noticed he had 10 Scion IQs (the one that is so small it looks like a Smart Car) in stock and they were not moving at all. With Scion, if you advertise a discount on one car you have to do it on every car because of their guidelines as a brand. We decided to run a one-pay lease. The customer paid a reduced price all up front that was bundled into a 24-month lease. We were able to get the price to $3,999 including all taxes, fees, and other upfront costs while only losing around $1,000 on the unit. We then advertised this heavily as, "Our best offer ever! Drive a Scion for $3,999 for two years." I am a firm believer that people will hear from an ad what they want to hear. But not in the last 25 years, probably not since the Ford Escort of the early '80s has there been a car that I can remember that sold for under $4,000. In addition to this being a great offer we emphasized the fact that there were 10 of these in stock. Telling the public there are 10 cars that are all less than $3,999 will drive a lot of traffic.

You can guess what happened next. There was a huge increase in traffic and while only one or two people actually took the one-pay lease deal, it still moved an extremely cold product. It helped the dealership out all the way around. This type of traffic was just looking for an inexpensive car.

In every instance noted these are real sales and real results. While they are all different brands and messages, they all share one thing in common: People believed all these offers were too good to be true, so they came to the dealership or went online to see for themselves. This is one of the ways you can be successful when dealing with cold merchandise.

2. Advertise your hottest products to move your coldest ones. This is the other way you can solve your aged inventory issues. Dealers often ask me what to do about a certain product that they only have a few of or don't have traffic coming in on, and my answer is always the same, "Hot traffic will solve cold merchandise." Obviously you hope you never find yourself with a scenario like the Pontiac or Cadillac dealers previously mentioned, but you will have the one-offs and smaller numbers of vehicles that you just can't seem to sell. The tactic I use with this is to continue to advertise what is the hottest for you and position your people and the physical setup of your lot to be at your advantage.

A perfect example is a Toyota dealer who has too many Avalons in stock and nobody interested in them. Considering that the Camry is the best-selling car in America, this dealer should advertise Camry in an aggressive way and then switch people to the Avalon on the lot. I do a lot of Toyota work and have seen the average age of the Toyota buyer continue to get older and older. What this Toyota dealer should do is section off his Avalon inventory in with his Camry inventory and show Avalons to customers who are looking for loaded-up or premium-model Camrys. It makes perfect sense: This should be a great "step up" car for someone who may want a little more. The same example can be used on Nissan with the Altima/Maxima. You can generate more traffic on an Altima than you can a Maxima. You can see which customers have the financial ability to buy a higher priced car or may simply want to have a slightly nicer car.

This principle doesn't just hold true for car models either. The same process works for light trucks and sport utility vehicles. Advertise what people want to buy the most in order to generate the most traffic out of the buying market that you can. Once you have them, focus on selling them what you have on the lot. Sales people and managers will be the biggest source of help in this area. Once the customer is on the lot and engaged in the shopping process, the salesperson will step in with the right amount of spiffs and incentives and sell the customer the car that pays the salesperson the most. Ultimately, the customer will end up with the car that he or she wants or can afford, but this way the salespeople are using their ability to show off products that would otherwise be sitting there with the doors never cracked.

9

SPIKES AND DIPS

The highest highs and the lowest lows have been experienced by everyone in this industry at some point in time and it can be an absolute roller coaster ride. The ups and downs are best described as spikes and dips and our focus is on three distinct areas where they are most apparent: monthly open and close, core product sales, and internet traffic. Each scenario comes with unique circumstances as to why it occurs and the challenge is identifying processes and taking the proper steps to avoid or reverse the trend.

LAST 10 DAYS DRIVES FIRST 10 DAYS

In the course of a month, I visit dozens of dealerships. Depending on the time of the month, the mood varies from gross indifference to euphoria. Forecasts became a reality in 2012 due to the increase of last 10 days of each month being especially strong in sales. The spike is the closing period of peak performance with an increased sense of urgency and intensity of focus to put every walk-up behind the wheel. And inevitably there is the dip—the first 10 days of the following month. Customer interest may still be plentiful, but all you hear is business is slow and traffic is off. We all love the spike; we must strive to skip the dip.

What is the cause of the dip? Is it the nature of the market, or the human nature of a sales force? The market has been conditioned to believe that the last 10 days of a month are the best time to buy. Google the question, "When is the best time to buy a car?" The number of responses when we searched was over one billion. The majority of those contributors say the end of the month is when a car dealer is the most vulnerable and in a must-sell mode. I suggest taking the time to research this best-time-to-buy question and you'll be astounded to read the so-called experts' advice.

Returning to real-world information and looking at dealership traffic numbers, there is not a huge variance by weekly counts. This is my definitive point: *Salespeople make the difference and control traffic probably more than you know.* Which leads me to ask the difficult question, "Is your sales team content with focusing on selling everyone the last 10 days compared to an equal number of customers in the first 10 days?" I am not saying these two 10-day periods will ever come close to flip-flopping in making your month, but a relatively good start is far better than adopting an "it's just not going to happen" attitude.

While watching the most recent Olympics, I saw time and again how important the start of the race was in winning a medal. To those who say, "It's not how you start but how you finish," I say, "Don't push your luck." Today, the average shopper will visit approximately two dealerships—that's a keep-you-awake-at-night number and a significant drop from visiting over five dealerships just six years ago.

The point your dealership needs to clearly grasp is that the customer coming to visit your dealership in the first 10 days may not be back for your anticipated big finish. The value in getting off the line well and striving to stay on pace the entire month is that it ensures that you will be there at the finish more often than not.

The repetitive emphasis on the importance of a good monthly start is a topic you need to discuss openly with your managers. Whether it's a kickoff, spiff or a swift kick, your team must work the market that is out there every day and appreciate that the sale closed in the first 10 days counts the same as the last sale to hit monthly bonus money. Is this elementary? Yes, but nowhere as painful as missing your forecast by one, which may have been a sale missed on the first day of the month. Earlier I mentioned that the mood can vary from delirious to dismal at a dealership depending on the time of the month. During those last 10 days, when it becomes obvious there is no hope of hitting your forecast, nobody wants to be there. To make that final stretch or a run for the big money, I encourage you to stretch your sales people right from the start.

ESCALATED SALES CREATE DEPLETED SPACES

The *good* automotive news is that right now almost every brand has a hot product—Camry, Cruze, Fusion, Altima, Sonata…the list goes on. Over the years it has been proven time and again that when you hit the market at the right time with a good marketing plan, hot vehicles can escalate both traffic and sales. I realize this is not news to you and hopefully you are currently experiencing the spike of hot product sales. But what I see at our most consistent dealerships is that good operators are definitely enjoying the action, but they are also keenly aware of and planning for the *reaction.* You need to be prepared for the dip that comes when your hot product is depleted.

Inventory management, awareness and anticipation are a function of good communication and ahead-of-the-curve planning. The rise and fall of hot products on your lot is clearly dictated by factory supply and consumer demand. But if your team has a green-light plan and moves into replenishment mode at the earliest indication of product shortage you can better survive until the next allotment. I know dealers who have standing orders to secure late-model core vehicles to offer as certified even while that particular product is plentiful and sales are just beginning to ramp up. This practice is especially beneficial as you near model year-end. (As an example, you could promote "2014 models" *without* saying "new" while advertising a lower price than the market was hearing.)

What's the most frustrated feeling for you in this business? *If I had them, I could sell them all!* It would be nice to have them all but proper planning will garner you significantly more than your fair share. Encourage your inventory managers repeatedly to take action before the day's supply number becomes a problem. Pick up the phone and call; work as hard to get one more on your lot as you would twenty. One advantage of analyzing inventory supply-and-demand regularly within your dealership is that your managers will create a network of options for those times when you either need vehicles or need to unload inventory. When you as a dealer are faced with the situation of accepting X number of hot vehicles but only if you take delivery of Y number of not-so-hot product, this unique knowledge should enable a wiser decision in terms of accepting the X *and* Y inventory.

To enjoy the spike and endure the dip of in-demand core product, you need to work relentlessly to have the processes that provide response sooner rather than later. The reason is obvious: Inventory is the one element that can dramatically affect both the opportunity for a good close on the lot and online. As one dealer told me, "I sell cars, not pavement!"

RISE AND FALL OF WEBSITE TRAFFIC

Gayle Rogers is our Digital Director at Strong Automotive Merchandising. After returning from a dealer meeting we had a very insightful conversation. In reviewing their Internet activity, Gayle noted we were seeing numbers higher on SEM and SEO than we had ever experienced before. By tracking these increases, we learned that Tuesday, Wednesday and Thursday were core days showing the highest visitor frequency. It was exciting to hear the goal we set for overall traffic was now in the rearview mirror and we were reaching traffic numbers we never knew existed. The Internet was spiking. But wait, there was more.

Gayle prefaced his next observation by bringing up Newton's Laws of Energy: For every action, there is an equal and opposite reaction. His point was that even though Internet activity grows significantly when the market is in hot pursuit of in-demand vehicles, you will not have the same visitor intensity 24/7/365. In other words, one gangbuster Internet month could be followed by a 10 to 15 percent dip in the next month. Even the Internet is vulnerable to a dip.

I then asked how this could be avoided. Gayle's answer validated what you would imagine, that even with a tool like the Internet it is critical to have a complete plan to utilize its effectiveness. You cannot rely on spikes generated by periods of increased market demand or eblast mailings for example. Instead, you need a complete Internet presentation including written and video content, connective links, social media presence and always-current information.

Regarding an up-to-date site, Gayle made a great point, "If you don't have it on your site, it doesn't exist!" One critical element of providing a site that consistently converts visitors into shoppers is 100 percent adherence to the policy of immediately posting vehicles, both new and used. This allows you to keep the ball rolling because you can reach out through other digital tools, such as Facebook, with a new post and direct even more shoppers back to your site.

No question about it, you are going to see more Internet traffic in the months ahead, and with more visitors the variance in "spikes" and "dips" could be even more dramatic. My recommendation to you as a dealer is given with the admission that I am on the Internet learning curve. Have the right people on your Internet team and require them to make observations/presentations in language everyone can understand.

Our Director of Digital has such keen insight because he is Google-certified and capable of scrutinizing an analytics report with ease. Could he interpret an Arbitron reach and frequency TV market analysis with the same skill that many dealers have? Probably not, and that is the point. Get hooked up with a specialist! The Internet is not unchartered territory—success stories abound—and evaluating why and how you are doing business or losing business cannot be guesswork. You must insist on a digital process that is made relevant in terms that can be comprehended by everyone in the Internet loop.

Our friend Newton had three Laws of Motion, and this is my favorite: An object at rest will stay at rest unless another force acts on it. If you don't have an Internet specialist who can give you a clear picture, get one; if you do, schedule tutorial time to get your arms around the Internet and make that stranger your best friend. Your showroom doors may be physically locked at night, Sundays and some holidays, but you are still open for shopping. The Internet and your understanding of all it can do is an object that should never be at rest.

PROCESSES, PLANS AND OTHER BRIDGES

Bridges are a tribute to ingenuity, an engineering marvel that gets us from here to there when without them the road would stop. In any discussion of the spikes and dips the challenge is how to bridge the gaps without falling to the bottom of the valley. By now you know my answer. Plan, put the plan in place and plan again!

We already mentioned some steps you can take in building your dealership bridge, but because every bridge is designed to the specific terrain, you need to assess what is going to work best for you. The processes within your dealership must reflect what can best motivate your sales team, best prepare for product shortages based on prior-year sales, and encourage the most effective Internet presence possible for your current and emerging market.

It all starts in your annual planning sessions. This is the time to take a critical look at direct mail as a traffic-generating tool for generating a big start to a month. There has been much debate about how effective direct mail can be both in terms of over-mailing and the resulting ROI. It is a fact that many dealers are enjoying great success with a regular mail program. Whether the letter presents a new car opportunity, an equity offer for the current vehicle, a service special or an anniversary private sale, the increase has been tangible regardless of when the mail dropped in a particular month. The same holds true for timely eblasts that present an advantage for immediate response. Take a long look at the calendar and pick weekends for marketing thrusts that bring traffic into your dealership when conditions such as inventory are optimum.

What is the biggest change I have seen in the placement of marketing dollars? The Internet and other traffic-generating tools beyond traditional electronic media. In looking over agency meeting reports for clients representing a variety of budgets, the number of new entries has increased significantly: Facebook, email, Internet videos, SEM, direct mail, and special finance TV offers. These tools are utilized by top-performing dealers who are not the biggest spenders in their market. Even more importantly, their budget decisions are not made via a knee-jerk reaction of trying everything that "seems" to work. Instead, they are working their plan and proving efficient where they most need to be effective.

Panic is not a good plan and should always be the last response. The unexpected surprises we have faced (and overcome), such as a weather-related event or vehicle recall, are always going to be there. Spikes and gaps are also going to occur, but devoting the time necessary to good planning with open communication and precision execution offers you a bridge design that you can build and do so within budget. Just like a roller coaster, the automotive business has its ups and downs.

10

THE FIVE TYPES OF GENERAL MANAGERS

In the modern-day dealership, the general manager truly is the determining factor in how successful or unsuccessful a dealership is going to be. What is now required of a general manager has changed, brought on by the proliferation of the Internet, the progressiveness of the manufacturers with extended service/warranty programs and the complexity of stocking and pricing used vehicle inventory. To put it bluntly, the general manager is in more control of the dealership's destiny than they have ever been before. Regardless of being a publicly held or privately held dealership, the demands on this position are greater than ever before.

Over the last 10 years, I have spent over 600 days going in and out of roughly 250 different dealerships all across the United States. This roster of dealerships includes just about every brand from high-volume stores to ultra-luxury stores; so many that I have already forgotten more than I can remember. But what this time and travel has taught me is that there are different types of general managers and no two are ever going to be identical.

General managers are almost always predictable in regard to what type of executions they will like and how long they will want to stay with them. With any type of advertising, consistency is the key and without it and the willingness to build momentum from it, no advertising plan is ever going to work. Through working with and watching so many decisions being made, I have formed the opinion that there are five types of general managers and with a few rare exceptions, everybody belongs to one of these categories.

THE OPERATOR

The Operator is by far the most consistent and most stable manager. He/she controls a more tenured staff, and has probably only worked for a few different owners/companies over a long period of time. The Operator is the poster child for consistency in all aspects of the business and exudes direct and unwavering decision making when it comes to everyday details. This is who, as a marketing company, you find to be the best partner to work with on a daily basis because you always know where you stand and what the most important task at hand is. They have generally stayed with the same brand for a number of years through ups and downs while maintaining a genuine belief that they sell the best brand in the world.

The strengths of this general manager are exactly what you would expect from the title. They command a strong grasp of all different areas of the business. They understand sales for both new and used cars, as that is what keeps them the busiest. There is also a great understanding of finance and they lead the direction of the store through a very strong finance director or Finance and Insurance (F&I) department. This person is not so shortsighted that he/she only pays attention to the front end of the business. While more of their time will be spent in the front end than the back, the Operator has very good control over the service and parts departments and uses this area to greatly bolster the profitability of the store. The Operator seeks out new opportunities for a store but does so in a slower more methodical way than most would.

In the last few years I have watched this type of general manager start customer rewards programs specific to their dealership, begin rental and courtesy car fleets, venture into special finance and buy here/pay here arms of finance, begin stocking and selling wholesale used cars, enter into the wholesale parts business, and most importantly, develop very high-powered Internet departments and Business Development Centers (BDC). All of these executions have been added to increase profits and drive more business through the existing dealership structure while this person dealt with the day-to-day, week-to-week business at hand.

This is by far the most consistent marketer out of all general manager types. They are very reluctant to change direction or strategy, and most of the time, will look inward just as much as outward if the results from their marketing are not what they want them to be. The Operator is always looking at new ideas and the latest technology. They can spot a sales pitch from a mile away and are hard to fool by something that is not solid or concrete. Most people in this category are die-hard believers in long-range planning and only make changes when absolutely necessary.

The only weakness that I have ever found with someone who fits the description of the Operator is their reluctance to let people go who have gotten stale. They are very loyal to their people—sometimes to a fault. Most who fit this description start in a dealership as a lower-level employee or manager and get promoted all the way to the top. Sometimes this creates resistance toward replacing current staff but the payoff is in the loyalty that this type of manager with this longevity brings to an organization. Other than being overly cautious to replace a long-time employee or manager, the Operator is one of the best categories for a general manager that can be placed in a dealership in the current climate.

THE FIXER

The closest classification to the Operator is what I have come to call the Fixer. The Fixer is always looking for what they and their team can do to be a better selling, better servicing, more profitable dealership. Usually you don't find this type of general manager in a current dealership; they are brought in from outside for either a culture change or organizational change that will increase the speed and profitability of the dealership. I have worked with a lot of these types of general managers, and the best way to describe them is to liken them to a crew chief of a racing team. The crew chief is the one who is always looking for a way to save an inch here or there, or increase one mile per hour by making a minor tweak to something on the racecar. The same holds true with the Fixer. They are always looking for an extra dollar or two in each department and are constantly pushing their people to be better than they ever thought they could be. Like the Operator, the person cast in the role of the Fixer has a firm command on all different aspects and businesses within a dealership. They understand sales, service, finance, parts, wholesale, administration and the Internet. This general manager has to understand all these areas because they are always solving problems that are resulting in more products sold and more profit retained by the dealership.

The single greatest strength that the Fixer holds is the ability to fix the broken. An owner or a public company never hires a fixer to come into a dealership that is running smoothly; in fact it is much the opposite. This role usually begins when a store is losing money, losing people, or losing market share to everyone in town. The Fixer is never hired to maintain the status quo. (It would almost be better to have a subtitle on their business card that calls them a "Shakeup Artist," because their job is to make comfortable employees uncomfortable if they are not performing.) As previously noted, this general manager knows all aspects of the business and focuses on areas that are going to turn profit around the fastest. They are also quicker in their decision-making than most because even if what they want to try doesn't necessarily work out, it is still better than what they currently had.

The Fixer believes that people make the difference but will not hold onto somebody for a second if they think there is a better choice for the position out there. More often than not the Fixer usually ends up with a new, well-recruited choice to run the back end of parts and service; it can be easier to change an attitude by changing a body rather than placating to an ego. Regardless of the department, when a Fixer enters into a dealership or a new job it might as well be posted on the walls of the dealership that all employees must re-interview for their jobs and the Fixer is taking applications this very minute.

Changes are usually made to advertising and marketing pretty quickly. This general manager is usually in this role because they have turned around previous dealerships. They usually have a game plan for how they should market. But just like not wanting to wait around with employees, oftentimes the Fixer will try out new things quickly to see how they work. They know that even if it fails, the result will be better than if the changes were not put into place. From an advertising standpoint fixing a dealership is a great opportunity. It allows you to work with a person who is not tied to any of the ways of old; there is a blank canvas with new ideas and a fresh perspective. Not all of the ideas generated turn into real executions, but it gives you the ability to stretch your legs creatively. You could almost call the Fixer an inventor. They are continually looking and tweaking because they are never satisfied. This is the guy that always wants more and never gives up. Just like the crew chief on a race team, this general manager is on a constant quest to improve and build.

THE NOMAD

To best describe the Nomad is to classify somebody that has made several moves in their automotive career. Whether the situation that caused this person to make multiple moves was based on events or just circumstances and luck always varies. But there are many general managers out there who wear the badge of the Nomad. Generally, they are not loyal to one particular brand. They don't mind moving to new regions or areas of the country if the right opportunity comes along. Some people reading this who are classified as Operators or Fixers may not be able to fathom this but there are general managers out there who have worked in 20 different jobs in 20 different years. The mere sound of that can be amazing, but trust me, I have seen it before and not just once or twice.

The Nomad usually doesn't have a 360-degree understanding of all the internal businesses that make up a successful dealership. If they understand sales then they usually are lacking in parts, or if they are steeped with a strong background in service then they are usually not on the cutting edge of sales. This person is best described as having a few things in dealership management that they can do really well and a handful of others that get neglected or seldom attended to. Most Nomads lack the structure that is given by a great mentor or teacher. In talking and working with this type of person over the years, they very seldom talk about who trained them and how they learned all the tricks of the trade. While the old-school era was mostly older dealer principals who took young, energetic guys under their wings, most people who fit the mold of a Nomad lacked that training and early career development, thus they lack the ability to sustain success. More times than not, they started out only focused on the goal of making money and not on mastering the true day–to-day operations of a retail automobile dealership.

Because the Nomad has moved around quite a bit in their career, they have most likely done just about every form of advertising that is out there. These people generally have run all types of media and all types of messages. They tend to think that each store, while different from the last one, needs a completely different strategy in advertising and marketing. What really happens in most cases is what I call "experimental marketing." This means wanting to try something new just because they are in a new place. Whatever advertising the store was doing before this Nomad arrived is almost always thrown out the window and something new is created for the store upon their arrival. Not saying it is a right or wrong thing to do, but very rarely do you find a Nomad who is going to keep the plan that was in place before they got there.

The single greatest reason that most general managers in this class end up getting hired is the ability to make a lot of money in a short amount of time. Again, most Nomads are pretty sharp in sales so they can take an underperforming store and increase sales volume and front end gross much to the liking of an owner of a public company. But they have a hard time sustaining it and being consistent month after month and year after year. Thus the reason for a short-lived tenure and a mindset that has this person looking for bigger and better things once the bloom has worn off the rose. Sometimes the Nomad can surprise even the toughest critic and find an organization and a dealership where they can land on their feet and really build a career, but more times than not, they get the itch to keep on moving. Their resume is probably in so many hands that even when they do find a home they continue to get calls because of the close relationship they have with their headhunter.

THE GYPSY

In describing the next general manager classification, think of the Nomad but add a couple of their closest friends and family members with them. You may laugh but it is true. In fact, they might as well just pull up in a motor home and park it behind the dealership, because they travel in packs. The Gypsy is the general manager who moves around from store to store, but always tells the owner of the dealership that they have a great team that is ready to follow at a moment's notice. This crack team of automotive all-stars usually contains somebody who can handle the service department, someone to work in finance, a washed-up sales manager or two, and most often, a BDC or Internet manager. This is the team concept that moves around from store to store with the hope and promise of being a total turnkey solution. Maybe it would be better to be called the, "Turn your key while we rob you blind" solution, but it is still always phrased as a solution.

Please do not get me wrong. A team of traveling Gypsies can make a positive impact on a dealership and its net profit but there is a lot of baggage that comes when this many people are brought into an organization. If the store has a staff of longtime tenured employees, most of them will either leave or get demoted if this type of general manager takes over. If they left somebody else to come work with you, then they will probably leave you to go work for someone else.

When it comes to advertising, just like having their own traveling team of people, the Gypsy's advertisers generally follow along as well. They are usually very tight and have methods that they are going to replicate based on success they have had in other markets and in other stores. Sometimes this general manager is very knowledgeable of successful marketing tactics, but it is hard to create long-term success because they are always pulling up stakes and moving to another town.

THE LOST

The last and most certainly least of the general managers out there is the Lost. The name truly does say it all as this general manager is in over his head when it comes to running the daily operations of the dealership. The problems that will be the demise of this person all start with their control over their people. The people who work for the Lost usually do not respect them or the direction that they are leading the dealership. This can easily be detected through the dissention in the ranks of department managers and those in the sales force. It can easily be transferred over to the owners and corporate managers who do not believe in the person or the direction they are being taken. When people don't respect the speed and strength of the boss, then there can never be a chance for success and profit for the store.

The Lost never have a handle on the entire workings of the

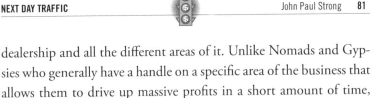

dealership and all the different areas of it. Unlike Nomads and Gypsies who generally have a handle on a specific area of the business that allows them to drive up massive profits in a short amount of time, this individual is directionless and doesn't have a chance at making one department work, let alone several.

When it comes to advertising and promoting, the Lost are the ones who waste hundreds of thousands of dollars a year in experimental advertising, and by the end of their careers they have wasted millions of someone else's money. While advertising is not the only place they create massive amounts of waste, it can be the most obvious. This type of manager will have no consistency in their message because they have no confidence in their plan of attack. Their approach to advertising is like most things they do and is flawed. Where a good manager will remain consistent with a strategy, the Lost will be the poster child for the knee-jerk reaction.

The general manager is the most important determining factor in how successful or unsuccessful a dealership is going to be. To be successful month in and month out, a dealership must be able to develop and build its momentum in all areas of operation—not just in advertising. Each type of general manager will have their own method and style of advertising. Some advertising strategies work better than others, some last longer than others, and some are destined to fail from the beginning. With that said, the one thing that is common with all of these general managers is they all believe in advertising as a means to finding traffic to grow a dealership's size and profitability. You could put it this way: If there is a type of general manager who doesn't believe in advertising then I wouldn't know what to write about him/her because I wouldn't have hung around them long enough to finish a cup of coffee.

11

THE EASIEST TRAFFIC TO DRIVE: SERVICE TRAFFIC

I n this chapter we will discuss one of the most overlooked sources of driving traffic to a dealership in the modern-day era. Far too often dealerships only look at ways to drive traffic to new and used car sales departments and forget about spending adequate dollars to drive service customers. As I mentioned earlier, I am a believer that your previous customers are your best source of new business but this chapter is going to address the need grow your customer loyalty and how to do it by increasing your fixed absorption.

The general public sometimes forgets that dealerships offer just as good, if not better, value than the independent or the franchised maintenance-only shops so it is crucial they be reminded constantly. Every dealership should send out enticing and appropriate service offers and specials to their owner body through a number of different channels. Every dealership should be discussing service marketing just as often as they discuss sales marketing. There is no silver bullet or instant headache pill that can fix a lack of service traffic overnight, but a steady and consistent plan over time can build your business by increasing your repair-order count month after month. Dealerships now have the ability to send out service offers or specials via direct mail, email, text messages, phone calls and plugs through social media outlets for little to no money. The problem is many dealerships have no long-term plan or strategy in place. I think there is a fundamental problem when any business has no overall goal and strategy for growing their previous customer base.

I have compiled a list of reasons dealers have given me over the years as to why they don't need to advertise service. Take caution before reading as the truth can either hurt or set you free!

1) The manufacturer has a program in place for us.

Sure they do. They all do. If you want the definition of a cookie-cutter or a one-size-fits-all approach, then let the factory do your job for you. How many times have you told a representative from your factory "my dealership is different" or "my customers are different"? If you let the factory dictate which programs you run and how often you hit your customer base, then your results will most likely be below average compared to your competition. There is no separation or plan of attack to take your business further and faster than your fellow brand dealers. Plus, the most irritating thing to me in service advertising is the factory-endorsed creative. It is all boilerplate artwork with the same offers that have a "dealer name goes here" mentality. There is no customization and therefore it says nothing about the personality of your dealership. All advertising should be a window into what goes on at your store. Service is no different. The piece should contain your logo, pictures of your waiting lounge, talk about your amenities and have a personalized note from either the owner or service manager. There needs to be a customized message that connects your customers back to your dealership. Without it, it's just another piece of junk mail or spam email.

2) Our service penetration is already high.

Unless you are recapturing 100 percent of your customers to be repeat-service customers your absorption is not high enough. Yes, I realize no dealer in the history of this business has ever achieved 100 percent and that is my point. You can never let up and never assume that you are getting all that you can get. Even if you are covering between 70 to 80 percent, you are still vulnerable. Plus, you can look at growing your share from other makes that you do not sell. Dealers are always looking to conquest the other vehicle in the driveway and this is a key area to focus on. If your service penetration is already high then you are obviously doing a great job with your brand. Look to other competitors to expand your brand and you will conquest these people to be sales customers over time as well.

3) Our shop cannot handle any more traffic. We are slammed as it is.

Congratulations! Call a construction company! Believe it or not I have heard this on more than one occasion and it still amazes me that people will let these words come out of their mouth. If you can't afford to expand or don't have space to add more service bays, then look at taking on a second shift or even a night shift. If your service department is already handling more than they can bear, then I am sure you are somewhat profitable. Imagine how much more you could make if you could increase your traffic by 20 percent annually in this department. If you actually tried to generate traffic then just think how much bigger you could grow. I have seen dealers do things like hire valet parking attendants to speed up the flow on the lane and get cars to the techs faster. Dealers have hired outside detail companies to be onsite and speed up car-wash time because their detail department couldn't handle all the work. A dealer I know even subbed out work to a struggling local tire shop when his tire sales outran what his team could get done in a day. If you do not want to build you can always outsource, but you should always try and maximize traffic, especially when it is easy to generate.

4) Our service manager doesn't like to get aggressive on pricing.

Great news! You don't have to give away the farm. Have your manager be the driving force behind packaging up compelling offers that still have great gross for the service department. The modern-day buzz word for this is "the bundle." We all know that oil, tires, batteries and brakes are the key elements that lead to the highest percentage of repair orders. If your team likes to hold gross then let them. Challenge them to come up with ways to pile multiple services into groups that give customers a reason to buy from you. This can come in many forms but when you have a manager that is resistant to give aggressive offers in order to drive traffic to your service lane, allow him the freedom to create something on his own that will work for how he wants to run the shop. Some stores that do not like to get aggressive on pricing often have an independent repair shop in town that is a giveaway artist, offering non-profitable deals in order to get traffic. You should be able to overcome this by being a reputable franchise dealership. Remember, you are the name brand and they are "brand X." You should be able to overpower and out-maneuver them. If you still cannot find a way to create competing offers, the factory is always running factory approved service specials. If nothing else, take their offers and copy them for yourself.

5) We need to fix our Customer Satisfaction Index (CSI) before we create any more traffic.

Find the people that are causing the CSI problem and eliminate them. You are holding back your business from growing and generating profit because someone on your service lane or in your department is not handling the work and your customers properly. Again, you may be in disbelief that people would say this but it really has become common: You do not stop advertising for new and used car traffic if you have CSI issues, so why should you stop advertising for service? Dealerships have created service business development centers and hired customer relations managers to handle customers in service. Both have worked well. Whatever the case may be,

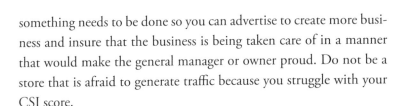

something needs to be done so you can advertise to create more business and insure that the business is being taken care of in a manner that would make the general manager or owner proud. Do not be a store that is afraid to generate traffic because you struggle with your CSI score.

6) I do not get paid on what the service department does.

This one only comes when a general manager/sales manager is in charge of making the advertising decisions and their compensation is not tied to the performance of fixed operations. If this is occurring, then you have two possible problems that need to be resolved. Problem number one is that the wrong guy is making the advertising decisions for the whole store. There should be one head and two bodies. Both the general manager/sales manager and the service manager must be in concert with each other so that all areas of the dealership are firing on all cylinders. Problem number two is that the general manager/sales manager may need a new pay plan or a change in attitude. Regardless of pay plan, every employee should be interested in seeing the store succeed, whether or not they are paid on it. That would be like the offensive side of a football team not caring if the defense stopped the other team from scoring. There is, without a doubt, a lot of greed in the retail automotive dealership today but if your store has this mindset, you have a major problem.

7) We need every advertising dollar to drive fresh sales business. Service is okay.

To use another sports analogy, "The best offense is a good defense." If you are struggling to get the volume you need in sales then the number one place you should look is your captive audience. The people currently servicing cars with you whose cars are 10 years old or less are your most captive audience. These customers already have a relationship with you and trust you enough to maintain their car (most of which probably purchased from you before). So why aren't you looking to them for pull-ahead offers? It is not as exciting for the sales department as running a promotion that brings in 100 fresh ups to the showroom on a Saturday, but it is an incredible source of business from people who have an established trust in the dealership. It takes more work to mine your customer base and conquest customers out of the service lane, but if you are looking for easy deals and great inventory to stock your used car lot, then this is the answer. I have heard people many times tell me they do not need to spend the money on service because all available dollars need to go to sales. I couldn't disagree more. To build both sides of the business over time you cannot neglect one area to solely focus on the other. It is necessary to promote both simultaneously.

Now that we have overcome every objection as to why you shouldn't advertise for service we will talk about the most effective ways to structure a plan that provides the most effective return on investment with your service advertising dollars. Remember, as stated at the beginning of this chapter, "Service traffic is the easiest traffic to drive," but it is a process that must be done consistently and effectively over time. Just like when people enter the market to buy a car, they are not always in the market to service their car. That's why you have to be there with great frequency so you do not get lost or forgotten by them. Here are the channels you need to focus on.

1) Direct Mail

There is no substitute for putting an advertisement physically into a person's hands, which can be done by sending them a piece of mail. A great deal of Americans will check their mail over their trash can, but at least you're making an impression on them before they throw you in the garbage. Just like sales customers, service customers may not be in the market to get service done at that time, but they see you and are reminded that not only do you sell cars, but you also service them. During the recent recession we helped our dealers become better marketers to their owners with a service message through the mail. The ones who took our advice grew their service business at a pace faster than the rest of the market.

The mail can come in many forms, from simple postcards to

personalized letters and even large multi-page coupon books. Regardless of the form they come in each of these executions will work to generate traffic to the service lane. The goal must be to stay in front of them constantly. The ideal frequency to mail your customers is once every 60 or 90 days. This frequency is the same whether they are considered active or inactive based on the standard driving patterns of Americans and service intervals recommended from most manufacturers.

2) Email

There is no doubt we live in a digital world where a person can learn anything simply by typing it into their phone and doing a search. People are addicted to email and check it constantly. Just like a physical direct mail piece, email advertisements can be considered junk mail but the key is that you can stay top-of-mind with your audience through your email offers. By having a reoccurring email message sent out to customers with service offers and specials you have used yet another channel to promote your service department and your latest offers and information.

With service email marketing programs, our company has created a plan around promoting the most attractive deals in the service department and maintaining a frequency that keeps us top-of-mind on a monthly basis. The advantage of an email blast is that it is low-cost. It only requires the manpower and effort of layout and scheduled distribution. This may seem like a simple tactic but too many dealerships do not pay enough attention to promoting their service department among their existing owner body. Because of this mindset, we have found that the best time to send out a service email blast is within the first five days of the month. For most manufacturers who change their incentives and objectives on a monthly basis, the respective dealerships are sitting on their hands the first couple days of a month while offers and content for incentive-driven advertising is put together. With service, there usually aren't many new incentives and programs that need to be reviewed so we take this time of the month to focus on sending a message to customers that pertains to service. We know from research sources and historical data that the first 10 days of the month are the slowest in the retail car business so if the market is not stirred up for vehicle sales then we can turn it up for vehicle service.

Service customers are what we call "need buyers" in that they have a need and handle that need when it happens. They are not like sales customers who have been trained that the best deals come at the end of the month or are waiting on the second paycheck of the month before they buy their new vehicle. Service customers come into the market when they look at their odometer and see they need an oil change or a repair light comes on in the car. That is why you can form an effective plan through email marketing if you focus on promoting service in the first ten days of the month.

The content of these emails needs to be very simple. Give the customer a reason to buy and a reason to buy "your service" from "your dealership." Create timely offers that focus on the needs of the customer at the given time. If the winter season is upcoming then have a "Winterization Special." Just prior to spring, have a "Spring Spruce Up." Also do not ever forget that oil changes, tires, batteries and brakes are the pillars of any service department and the lifeblood of how you will grow your service business. We have found it beneficial to include pictures of your service department staff so you see a familiar smiling face that will greet you when you pull your car in the service lane. People like to do business with other people and adding a personal touch to the content of the email can only help increase the conversion rate and amount of people who will respond to the offer.

3) Website

In the digital information age it is astounding to me how few dealerships will customize their service offers on the web. Just like with service direct mail, many people will say, "Well, the factory does that for us so we don't have to." My answer to that statement is,

"You are unfit to run the marketing for your dealership." If you settle for what the factory is promoting you will never be any greater than average. Your website needs to be a centralized source for information on and about service as well as specials and discounts that are currently being offered. There needs to be space dedicated to service on the homepage of the site as well as separate links to service and parts through the menu tabs of any website. Some dealers who have been very progressive in their thinking have even been able to create separate websites that are only for service and offer menus and competitive pricing for the public.

We have been able to generate enormous amounts of traffic to our dealerships' service lanes simply by creating custom content on the service pages of a website. There is no reason not to take advantage of this free digital real estate and make the offers and content unique for your store. Your website is your own personal space to promote offers, coupons and specials that will generate traffic. The emphasis on creating traffic from a captive audience on your website needs to be thought of the same way for service as it is for sales. There needs to be content that is timely. The offers need to be aggressive to generate traffic and separate yourself from the other dealers and independent service providers. You can also tie in these pages from your website to service offers that are sent out through email and posted on other digital sources. This will only help increase your traffic by having all current offer information on your website.

4) Text Messaging

The proliferation of text messaging in the last five years has been nothing short of amazing. The amount of people that would rather just send a text than call and have a conversation is growing rapidly every day. You need to be able to adapt with this change in communication. Most CRM (customer retention management) tools now have texting options and capabilities for you to communicate with your customers. This is a great tool to utilize if you are not already taking advantage of it. There is some old-school thinking that dealers and managers believe: "Customers do not want to get a text message from us, it is intrusive." If you think like this you will be left behind. Now is the time to get out in front of the texting generation and make sure you are using this as it is another free way to communicate with your existing owner body.

Text messaging should be thought of as a means to "up-sell" service to customers once they are already in your lane, as well as a way to reconnect with inactive service customers who are not responding to mail, email or your website. A person's telephone is now the most important device they carry, and it is an instant way to touch people and get immediate action. Your offers cannot be as detailed and intense with texting as they can be with mail and email, so keep it simple. Either tell the person it is time for them to come in for a service visit or give them an incredible offer that is sure to drive traffic.

5) Service BDC (Business Development Center)

You have seen them now for over a decade in the sales department and just like everything else, the BDC is slow to make its way over to service. Most dealerships are not calling missed service appointments like they do missed sales appointments. Most dealerships do not get as excited about the number of service appointments on a Saturday as they do the number of sales appointments and this is where the disconnect occurs. Service customers and the process of generating and maintaining traffic need to be thought of in the same terms for service as they are for sales. I have had the privilege of working with dealerships that run a great service BDC and the difference it can make is incredible. I have even witnessed the transformation of dealerships that didn't have a service BDC that started one and saw their traffic and profits grow.

The service BDC is responsible for setting and following up on appointments as well as reconnecting with lost souls from the department. No matter what franchise in what city, every dealer that I have ever met wants to get more of their lost souls back in for service. They will spend stupid money to go after these people through mail and email programs yet they are slow to invest someone from their dealership in making calls and sending emails to these customers to bring them back into the dealership. A well-trained and managed service BDC staff can be an incredible financial windfall for any dealership. Consider the profit opportunity with this traffic-generating machine sitting right under your own rooftop. You could increase your service business by 20 percent in the next 12 months and make your technicians and managers more effective with their time. The possibilities are endless and the naysayers are abundant. Be aggressive and go after the business that you are losing on a daily basis out of your service department.

6) Mass Media

Many people think advertising service in any form of media is a waste of money. To people who think this, all I have to say is, "Look at Pep Boys, NAPA, Tire Kingdom, Firestone, and every other service center that is out there today." These businesses, just like yours, thrive on traffic. Most of their customers purchased a car from you or one of your local competitors. Television, radio, billboards and even print still prove to be effective forms to generate service traffic. Don't think that you can produce a sales ad and simply tag it with a service offer—it isn't that easy. To make these ads effective they need to be dedicated to service only; they need to promote a service not a sale. Thinking that you shouldn't spend media money on service is like thinking you could play basketball wearing a pair of flip-flops. You could try it, but you are going to lose every time.

Dealerships that have allocated money to promote service departments have seen gains in net profit by increasing their absorption rates and their monthly repair order counts on a continuous basis. Whatever message that you decide to run must be communicated throughout the dealership and there must be a steady stream of parts and personnel to handle the traffic it will drive. This is a very easy and effective way to drive incremental business and profit to any store. Just like all the other methods mentioned in this chapter, offers via media must be ultra-aggressive and able to be delivered once someone shows up at the dealership. A lot of manufacturers even offer special co-op reimbursement if you promote service through mass media, which is even more of a reason to do it since you can get credit back for the money spent.

7) Digital

Just like with mass media advertising, many people who are involved with making the media decisions for service overlook the fact that customers are constantly looking online for automobile service. There is very little attention and effort placed on search engine optimization and pay-per-click ads from a dealership with service content. I think this is simply because new and used car sales take the top priority and by the time people have adequately done a good job in these areas they simply overlook the fact that service needs to be factored into the equation. This needs to be monitored and corrected if you ever want to grow your service business past the point of status quo.

Every paid search or optimization campaign that a dealership runs needs to have a focus on service. You can break it out into a separate dollar amount or budget if that makes it easier but it needs to happen in some way, shape or form. The same offers that have been mentioned in this chapter need to be addressed when you are trolling for traffic online with your service offers. Focus on very aggressive hooks that will entice people to click on your ad. Keyword research through Google, Yahoo, and Bing will show you are the most searched service terms in your area and this is a good place to start. Look at what people are looking for in their searches and craft your offers to be appealing to these people. Digital advertising dollars are currently returning the best return on investment of anything available and it is no different for service. This needs to be implemented as part of the service marketing plan and continued on an ongoing basis.

To bring this section of service marketing to a close, I believe without a shadow of a doubt that service traffic is the easiest traffic to drive to a dealership. Most dealerships service ten times more cars than they sell in any given month and there is a reason why. People are more interested in taking care of their cars today than ever before and more trusting to a franchised dealership than a local independent repair shop. The reasons why dealerships don't promote service are abundant and very present in today's automotive world. But there are just as many ways that you can promote service as noted in this chapter and each one of them I have seen as a proven and effective method. A dealership that has a healthy and thriving service business will be far more profitable than a dealership that offers mediocre service and lackluster care. While oftentimes the focus in generating traffic falls on the sales side, service cannot be overlooked.

12

CLEAN UP IN THE SERVICE LANE

The first time I visit a new dealership it always begins with a facility walk-around. I usually request the general manager or owner to give me the tour. During a recent excursion through a very well-run store with a huge service center, I asked how many service customers they received on average each month. They average 3,500 customer repair orders a month, a pretty amazing amount. That means even on a slow day this store still has over 100 people on average coming in for service. On a fast and furious day that number may climb to over 200.

What really stood out to me about this particular service center was the fact that with thousands of customers in and out each month, their service area was spotless. This dealership was four years old but looked like it had just opened yesterday. It was refreshing to see that everything was kept in tip-top condition with nothing out of place or dirty.

Let me first establish the premise of why you must create a mind-set in your dealership to "clean up in the service lane." The two parts of this chapter will take you through how customers perceive your dealership as a service center and the endless opportunities for new sales business that are sitting in the service lane.

More and more we get requests from our clients to promote their service business through direct contact channels of mail and email, while adding specials, coupons and pricing menus to their dealership websites. A big push recently has also been to promote the fact that the dealership services all makes and models. This could be the realization that the average age of vehicles still hovers well over 10 years. So owners are scheduling service to keep their vehicle on the road for a while longer—and that is the key. Or, this could be the realization that to truly grow your dealership profitability on an ongoing basis in the current economic climate, you are going to have to drive more service business. Your service department is doing business every day with people that can clearly be identified as a captive audience *and* a potential source of new or used sales revenue. This cannot be ignored.

While this book focuses on next day traffic and turning shoppers into buyers, the downturn in the economy from 2008 to 2011 has taught me to focus on the everyday returning customer body as a place to mine extensively for "created traffic." I have said it before and firmly believe the service lane may be the most overlooked place in our industry for fresh customers. The previous chapter talked about service traffic being the easiest traffic to drive, and without question, these two were put back to back for a reason. Creating more service traffic leads to more opportunity to conquest business out of your service department. While every store will vary in the amount of daily repair orders that it writes, the one thing they all have in common is repeat and conquest customers. Customers pass through the dealership every day in the service department. Members of the sales department should capitalize on the opportunity to make them sales customers.

I have used this phrase to identify this point further: "Your service drive is your own private vehicle auction, and you are the only one who is invited." Dealerships spend thousands of dollars a month so that their used car managers and used car buyers can travel to auctions all over the country. This money doesn't even count the auction fees and transportation fees that they have to pay once they find the cars and bring them back to the dealership. Not to mention the fact that titles get lost, keys are misplaced and many other heartburn issues which are created by having to go to auction to find your used car inventory.

Most of the time when attending an auction, the goal is to bring back the same brand that your dealership sells as new cars. Why go to auction and incur travel expenses and time spent away from the dealership when you have the single biggest opportunity to find quality trade-ins right in your own service department where it's easier to control costs? When you follow a plan to make a sale by trading up a service customer in service, you are not held to a bidding war with other dealers and wholesalers as at auction. You can make an offer that most times can be structured in a new car deal to hold more gross profit. While it is simple, it takes skill and diligence to execute properly. It can be an incredibly profitable way to generate even more business out of an already busy and profitable department.

Service-lane selling is an age-old tactic. It usually consisted of an over-achieving sales associate who got to the dealership early and worked the service lane and waiting area by talking to customers about trading out of their vehicle. It is a tactic used by some sales people on a consistent basis if they have a loyal following of customers who constantly come in for service. Sometimes a sales force will focus on it if they are trying to meet a month-end quota or hit a certain objective number, but very rarely is the service lane a regimented part of the advertising plan. The point of all of this is that it *should* be used and practiced on a day-to-day basis in every dealership whether you write 35 repair orders a month or 3,500.

There are many ways to notify service customers of the dealership's interest in their trade. It can be from a simple email message, signage in the service lanes, follow-up call centers after a service, or even hiring and placing people on the lanes to ask customers directly if they want to trade. The options are endless and the tools and technology exist through many different programs and providers. A dealership can literally start and build its own program to meet its needs. Our dealers have executed numerous tactics to create new sales out of service customers. Most all of them have generated success. Just like anything else, some stores have worked the program better than others. This tactic has sold a lot of vehicles and increased customer retention at a time when both of these things were very hard to do across the industry. Right now, most manufacturers are telling their dealers that the new buzzword in their language is "retention." Automakers are doing the math and realizing what a miniscule percentage growth in current customer retention will do for their dealers and their bottom line. They are running at it full speed ahead.

What if instead of trying to grind out a few more miles with their current car, a customer brings in his or her car for service because they are getting that car cleaned and tightened up in anticipation of a trade? What if that same customer bought their vehicle across town from your biggest competitor but was utilizing your service department for its location? You now have a conquest customer who likes your service but just didn't buy from you. I feel it is imperative to say if that customer decided to be a part of your next day traffic because they liked the treatment in your service department, you would call that a home run! Or when the owner of a vehicle brand that you *don't sell* decides to give you their business on a different vehicle because of what they have experienced as a service customer from the other car in their driveway that you *do* sell. That is an incredible win as well.

There can be no question when the moment comes for your service-only customer to purchase their next vehicle that your total service operation and experience is perceived as a bridge, not a blockade. People have strange mindsets and thought patterns. While they may service their car with you that they bought from someone else, in the very instant they get ready to buy, you may not have top-of- mind consideration for sales. That customer may think of you as a great place to get an oil change or have maintenance done, but they may think of somebody else when it comes time to buy. Remember, people are creatures of habit. They believe what they are told, and are influenced by what they hear from the public and their peers. Just because they are in your store today does not mean that they will be back tomorrow. Just because someone bought a vehicle from you does not mean they will ever even consider you for service regardless of what retention program your manufacturer comes out with and advertises to the masses. The new era of the car business will require you to turn your service department into a bridge for greater customer retention and endless conquest opportunities.

If you think everything mentioned in this chapter up to this point can be done with the flip of a switch then you are wrong. The next part of cleaning up in the service lane comes from how people perceive your service lane. Having a great service department is the foundational element to be able to create vehicle sales out of your service department. If the department is not one that attracts customers but rather one that deters them, then everything mentioned above is impossible. If the service department does not provide a great atmosphere then you can forget about pulling people out of their cars and putting them into a new one. If the service area is not run with serious attention to detail then you will be facing a hostile customer when you attempt to present sales options to them rather than an agreeable customer who is willing to listen to what you have to say.

In my thinking, a service department of professional people who take pride in their working environment with a "How can we help you?" attitude is the *only* option if you want a shot at moving your captive audience into the owner body column. All dealerships must fight to keep their customers every day and employ excellent service tactics. There are plenty of people who would love to get your oil change business, or your tire business, even your collision center business, if you slip up and make one mistake or treat one customer the wrong way. Most likely there is somebody in your market who is selling vehicle service cheaper than what you are offering. Because of this, you are always going to be in a constant battle to win over your customers by being an efficient and precise professional. Customer perception is critical to turn any service department into a funnel for vehicle sales and newly found traffic.

Some people say it is because I am a neat freak, but I cannot stand to walk into a service lane or waiting room that is dirty. It is one of the biggest turnoffs, especially after spending advertising money to generate traffic *and* pay a service manager plus an entire staff to settle for an unattractive service facility. Are you going to put all this effort into inviting customers into your business only to have them sit in a dirty, out-of-date service department? To win the customer over, in addition to a great professional staff, you must have the setting to back it up. People who want bad coffee and uncomfortable chairs can go to independent shops without the amenities. You are in the business of selling an experience as well as a service. The facility you operate in is as critical as the actual operations itself.

You know how it works, the better the experience with a business, the more eager you are to do business again. This is a connective process that you as a consumer apply every day in your personal choices. From the restaurants you frequent to the dry cleaner and the grocery store, there is a perception checklist that defines who keeps your business. I could rattle off a list of words but I think it is safe to say the final criteria always gets down to the umbrella term "attention to detail." To say it's the little things almost sounds superficial, but when it involves a money-spending decision, those extra touches are what sway many a consumer.

People who have bad experiences with businesses not only avoid them like the plague, but in today's world, they will flock to their social media site of choice and destroy that business' reputation in the eyes of their friends and followers. Businesses have to be more mindful today of negative reviews and feedback because of Facebook,

Twitter, blogs and forums. Dealerships are no different than any other service or maintenance business. An unhappy customer can go to a review site and blast you for even the smallest mistake. No, this will not kill your business but as much time and money that you spend defending your reputation, it is a major setback when someone blasts you for bad service or dishonest efforts and it is there for the whole world to see.

I hope I have made it clear how important the appearance and operation of any department frequented by customers is to your dealership, especially those that see dozens of visitors every day. Earlier I mentioned my visit to the well-run dealership that turned big service numbers. To my eye they clearly had a well-run, well-kept facility managed and staffed by people who took pride in the efficiency of the service processes.

Unfortunately there is a downside to that story. It clearly illustrates that even though you out-spend your competition on media, there is no amount of advertising that can overcome poor perception. If the customer is not handled in a professional manner when they arrive and not offered a great physical environment to wait, all of your efforts can easily be squandered.

Case in point: I work with a dealer who is great in his front-end business and enjoys sales numbers that reflect a well-executed plan. Over a period of three years this dealer gained an average market share of two percentage points per year against his metro-dealer competitors. He won every award and honor possible but there was one little thing that kept his dealership from being an unstoppable success: They were losing service customers at a faster rate than the competition and it could clearly be traced to the perception of their service department. This dealership was outselling everybody in new cars only to be losing customers from years back due to poorly executed service. In this scenario, the dealership sold vehicles well outside the market area it was responsible for with its manufacturer. That means the chance of defection in service is higher because people will have to drive farther just to have their vehicle serviced by the dealer. The competition does have a newer facility but even that could be overcome with attention-to-detail by our dealer in the overall appearance of the facility and the effort by employees. They had become content to let their captive audience sit in outdated furniture with drab colors and minimal amenities. There are hospital waiting rooms with more personality than this dealership.

Yes, they were bringing in first-time shoppers and converting them on the floor, but the service experience was a very real blockade that had customers saying no to long-term dealership loyalty. Even though this dealership outran the competition in gaining new customers from an aggressive advertising plan, they were losing a higher percentage of their existing customer base from a poorly executed service operation. This is what I call a "Net Some Game." Somebody is going to win and somebody is going to lose, you just better make sure you win at a faster pace than the other guy or else you are in trouble.

The service department is the epicenter of a captive audience—real people who are in your dealership. The term "unique visitors" as it applies to your Internet shoppers is probably getting more attention than the physical visitors just down the hall. Are you impressing them or making a bad impression? As the owner or general manager, how many hours out of how many days do you spend in the service department talking to and working with customers? How many times do you walk through your service department during peak traffic hours making sure everyone is being handled? I bet the answer is far fewer times than you stand on the showroom floor when customers are everywhere and the sales department is hopping. That's the question and here is your assignment: Grab a pen and paper and tour your service department right now, not as the owner or general manager, but as a service customer. Drive up just like a service customer, ask a service writer to do an oil change or wheel alignment and follow in the footsteps of your service customer.

What should be on your checklist?

Service Drive-up

- Neat appearance—the wow factor starts here, as in no cigarette butts on the concrete and no clutter blocking the drive
- Directional signage clearly defined
- Landscaping up-to-date
- Spotless floors/clean windows
- Easy access for customer vehicle entry
- Early-bird signage visible
- Special offers and promotions displayed where they can be seen
- Menu prices where they can be seen

Service Writers (and remember it's what you see at first glance)

- Professional in appearance, with the emphasis on *pro*
- Warm welcome delivered eye-to-eye as a front-line dealership representative
- Efficient but courteous in establishing rapport and identifying service need
- Orderly work stations
- Service Specials POP and presented to customer as savings opportunity
- Approximate time of delivery given to customer; identify customers who stay or leave
- Paper floor mats/seat protection put in place
- Ask for the best way to be contacted
- Directed to waiting area and informed of amenities

Service Customer Lounge

- Seating area in order (chairs in good repair, lights working)
- Current POP for Sales & Service specials present
- Coffee/refreshment area clean, well supplied—get a cup for yourself
- TVs working properly and not out of date; Wi-Fi operating

- Wastebaskets available and emptied regularly
- Restroom facilities clean, well supplied
- Periodicals and newspapers available
- Vending machines filled with variety
- Literature about your brand or dealership displayed
- Paging system clearly understood
- Restaurant area (if applicable) - Super clean in every aspect

SERVICE AREA OBSERVATIONS

If your actual service bays are visible to customers the effort must be made to keep up the appearance. For many of your customers, their impression of a service department may vary from the two-stall garage at the corner gas station to the NASCAR space-age mechanics they see on TV. Remember, in the back of their mind they are thinking about the premium they are paying to have their vehicle serviced at your dealership. Also, observe how your staff interacts with each other and the speed at which they move. Are their voices raised when giving instructions, do they ever look frustrated with part of the process, do they look excited and energetic? I assure you the dealership that was writing 3,500 repair orders a month had a staff that appeared to be moving fast. For that size business, how could you not be quick on your feet and be hustling to get the job done?

I also have an appreciation for the benefits of having the best mechanic in town on your service team and allowing them more leeway in how they perform their magic. More than one general manager has admitted they gladly leave the service team to the service manager. At the same time, the good operators know who the players are in their service department and maintain an open communication channel. It goes without saying that when something needs to change in the back regarding appearance, process, or whatever, it will be more easily facilitated when you have your top gun supporting the decision.

It is also a good practice for your staff to make sure the customer understands what you offer in regards to your service operation. I am not talking about the "vehicle delivery process" that all dealers participate in just so they don't get penalized by the manufacturers based on customer surveys, but truly and clearly selling the value of what you offer in terms of a world-class facility for them to maintain their newly purchased investment. Whether it is air-conditioned service bays or the experience of ASE Certified Mechanics to state-of-the-art technology available, selling your service area for what it is before the customer comes in will often create a more positive perception. Many dealerships conduct New Owner Service Clinics on a periodic basis and this is a great time to present your service facilities during non-business hours. But remember you are not going to get 100 percent attendance to this event. So every customer must be sold while they are still in the dealership before they leave with their new vehicle. Take advantage while they are in the euphoric state of just buying a vehicle and firmly back up what a great decision they have made to do business with you.

NEXT STEPS

What do you do after you have walked in the shoes of your service customer and thought more as a dealer about the opportunity that lives inside your service department to grow sales? Set up a meeting with key dealership personnel keeping in mind what staff members will need to be present to insure buy-in if changes are in order. You could even start by making an outline of what the biggest turnoffs in your service department are. This will shed real light on why people may not be coming back to you for service. Then you introduce the concept of a captive audience to the sales team and the impact this group can have to your monthly sales volume. For the entire dealership team, you marry this all together by painting a picture of a "dealership first" mentality and change their perception of what a fully functioning service operation could bring to the overall bottom line of your dealership.

If there has been zero synergy between your sales and service teams, then this has to be a well-planned meeting that includes both departments simultaneously, or else you will never see a cohesive effort between the two. Both groups have to see the opportunity that the service department has to impact positive change on the overall dealership. Obviously setting the bar to raise their game will require you to set some monetary rewards, but I do not know anyone who is not willing to pay people more if they can exceed goals and expectations. Set benchmarks for the service department to clean up their physical appearance and professionalism with customers, and set benchmarks for the sales department to engage with service. This has to be sold as something where the whole dealership stands to grow faster and with a better base of business than anyone else you compete with in the market, which is better for everyone's career in the long run.

I have stepped foot in many dealerships all across the country, and very few operate as efficient as have been described in this chapter, with an immaculate attention to detail in the service lane while having a cohesive "dealership first" effort between sales and service. The end-game of this exercise is to remind your entire team that a back-to-basics evaluation is both beneficial and necessary to maintain a high level of performance. The concept of attention-to-detail is good business, not a disciplinary move, and establishes a level of professionalism that employees will appreciate and customers respect.

Clean up in the service lane to clean up more bottom-line business. I have watched dealers spend millions of dollars executing programs to take care of their existing customers and to conquest new ones. So much money has been spent while so many people have been overlooked who are sitting right under your nose. I believe this is a concept you can enjoy as a business owner/operator and appreciate from an operations standpoint. More than once I have heard the positioning statement "service after the sale" as a selling point. My point is when service leads to a sale you undoubtedly have a dealership hitting on all cylinders.

13

CONNECTING THE DOTS

Every element of a dealership's annual marketing plan is critical because it's the foundation for driving next-day traffic. The basics, the "dots" as I have come to call them, are the bedrock of sustaining profitability in spite of any circumstances. Connecting these dots is a never-ending challenge requiring exceptional execution to insure each component compliments the other. Maybe the most critical element in connecting the dots is timing, and just like in many other industries and situations, we often learn that timing is everything. This is why I am putting the cart before the horse and telling you how this chapter ends before you finish the first paragraph: Plan annually instead of by the seat of your pants to afford more time to focus on merchandising and executing instead of, "What should we do now?"

Over the past few years, the automotive industry has been an uneasy economic prediction at best. We have been dealt surprises from vehicle recalls to natural disasters with the story inevitably becoming a national headline. We have seen heads of automakers called before Congress and bombarded with ridicule for decision-making as well as the second-guessing of whether a government-funded bail-out should be granted to keep their businesses alive. The presidential election of 2012, which many political experts say hung largely on Ohio voters and their strong ties to the auto business, is just another token of the power of the industry when it is amplified by the media. The business of selling, trading and servicing new and used cars is as much a high-stakes game as it has ever been, and that is before you factor in some of the ripples created by the news media and how they can affect business with their market influence. I know of no one who foresaw the far-reaching effects of the tsunami in Japan, Hurricane Katrina or Superstorm Sandy in 2012. But let me tell you what I did see in dealerships all over the country during these disruptions.

Following the tsunami, dealers whose annual plan included consistent direct mail and customer email blasts went to work with a well-maintained and managed marketing plan to their owner body. They worked service customers to create new revenue channels and all customers were wooed with almost unreasonable sounding offers for their current vehicle, just so the dealers would have used cars to sell.

And as soon as power was restored following Superstorm Sandy, several of our Northeastern dealers were out front in sending e-blasts advising their customers that the dealership was up and running and ready to assist them in the purchase or lease of a new vehicle to replace those damaged in the storms. Hard-sell creative spots were transformed to, "We are open extra hours and have power, coffee, and a place for you to charge your cell phone or computer," in a matter of minutes, which resonated well to a stressed audience during a crisis. These dealers had originally planned for campaigns and creative to tout year-end sales, so all they had to do was tweak the message and execute delivery to create a response far exceeding expectations.

I witnessed how dealers with a sound media plan already in place covering their markets could simply make a phone call to our company and change a price/item merchandising campaign to a Vehicle Replacement Center campaign in less than 24 hours. The ability to change and adjust at the speed of light was because the media plat-form was already built. The only change that had to occur was the flick of a creative switch and a brand-new campaign could begin immediately. The only thing that had to be changed was the execu-tion. The dealership knew where the dollars were going to be spent before these events occurred. The target was already predetermined; all that had to be done was a minor adjustment to the message. This would have never become a reality if these dealers were planning on a week-to-week or month-to-month basis.

The day-to-day operation of a dealership is stressful, competitive and right now, probably more liquid than ever before in history. Connecting the dots today is a far cry from the '80s and '90s, when the dealer who coordinated a sales event with TV, radio, and full-page print ads as well as balloons, hats and posters was considered a marketing genius. And truth be known, that dealer was ahead of the curve back then because having the thought process to tie an event together of that ilk required both planning and execution.

Today, however, a plan such as the one detailed above would be effective but old school, because it failed to cover the website, search engines, optimization, social media, behavioral targeting and experiential marketing channels that influence today's buyers. Very possibly the event executed with only the traditional components will still work and deliver a lot of traffic. However, there's no ques-tion that you are leaving too much on the table if all the bases are not covered. One reason you plan on an annual basis is to beat the clock when the time comes to execute an event. You simply have too much work to do to get the event up and running and there is not enough time to connect the dots even if you wanted to.

Your website—your virtual dealership—has the tools to provide unprecedented power for the immediate delivery of your message far beyond traditional boundaries. Imagine a planning meeting where your advertising agency says, "We have TV, radio and print ads as well as balloons, hats and posters for this sale." Most dealers that I know would ask me where the rest of the material is. Is that all we have to put behind this sale? What about home page graphics on the website, an owner body email blast plus a conquest email campaign? Does our Google pay-per-click copy play up the event? Do we have a special landing page built for this event? Who is in charge of updating Twitter and Facebook before, during and after the event? Does the digital welcome screen in the service lounge have our event creative? Have we printed and handed out flyers to local credit unions and banks? The challenge for reaching the total market in today's world requires planning on two levels. Combining the physical plan and the virtual plan connects *all* the dots that intertwine these two distinct but compatible levels for maximum return.

When you consider the different sources your potential customer relies on for shopping information, the dynamic of the automotive playing field has changed completely. We now have a term that media auditing firms are using called "the multi-screen viewer." This is an individual who may be sitting at home watching TV, while playing on a phone or computer at the same time. This suggests that marketing is now two-dimensional. I firmly believe a media marketing plan focused primarily on the physical *or* the virtual alone, even if it encompasses all 360 degrees of available tools, is influencing only a portion of your potential next day traffic. The successful annual plan going forward is a two-dimensional dynamic encompassing 720 degrees to reach more people than ever before. This ensures that your *total* market has exposure to your message wherever they are looking. Even though the online shopper right now may be the sweetheart of our industry and often referred to as the low-hanging fruit by most manufacturers and marketers. A plan that only targets this audience will miss a large part of the market. There are without a doubt massive numbers of viewers who are still influenced by television, radio, print, direct mail and point-of-sale materials that make up the physical dimension. Coming directly from someone whose livelihood and reputation live and die from the traffic that is created through advertising, you must have both dimensions!

The best illustration to depict my rationale in achieving connectivity between the physical and virtual dealership is to visualize a railroad track, two parallel lines with crossties. Every marketing effort, whether it is ongoing merchandising, a special event or a unique opportunity must be designed to travel between the tracks and tie in for recognition. Here are a few examples:

ADVERTISING YOUR MOST POPULAR VEHICLE AT A SPECIFIC PRICE
- Television with prominent URL identification
- Ad vehicle in showroom "As Seen on TV"
- Service Department and Showroom POP

<u>With</u>
- Website home page graphics reflecting TV design, "click here for inventory" button
- Email blast to owners/conquest list presenting special purchase opportunity
- Pay-per-click ads designed to capture online shoppers' searches
- Behavioral and retargeting ads with exact offer
- YouTube walk-around of vehicle
- Social Media promotion confirming value/legitimacy of the deal

72-HOUR USED SALES EVENT PLANNED TO COINCIDE WITH PAY PERIOD AFTER THE 15TH
- Television or radio with urgency, reason to buy now
- Vehicles marked and parked (with 72-hour sale tags)
- POP in showroom, service lane
- Postcard to owner body for private pre-sale shopping opportunity
- Phone operator inquiries, "Are you calling about the 72-hour sale?"

With

- Website home page graphic with dates, price points, "shop inventory now" button
- E-blast to positive equity owner body to pre-shop with link to "special" inventory
- Call center/BDC calling unsold customers over last 90 days announcing the sale
- Adjusted content and copy for pay-per-click ads
- Behavioral and retargeting ads showing that time is running out for the sale
- Social Media supporting scope of event, the savings, the excitement

SEASONAL SERVICE SPECIALS (SPRING MAILER FOR SUMMER, FALL MAILER FOR WINTER)

- Service mailer sent to service customers (owners and lost souls)
- Banners and posters in the service lane
- Offers posted in service customer waiting room (including copies of mailer)
- In-house memo to service writers to inform customers of specials/savings
- Phone operator asking callers if they are calling about the specials

With

- Website home page graphics listing specials
- Email blast to customers with special offers
- Landing page with most popular coupons listed
- Blog detailing importance of servicing car because of seasonal climate change
- Pay-per-click ads to cover money-saving service search
- Social media offering seasonal driving tips and inclusion of these offers

These examples cover the "kitchen sink" approach to marketing but are done so to illustrate that a 720-degree annual plan requires proper allocation of marketing dollars and executional attention by all parties participating. There must be a high-level of communication and timely execution of all the details or else you are going to miss your shot to reach a portion of your audience. But more than anything, the two-dimensional marketing model clearly shows why time must be set aside to concentrate on preparing your blueprint for optimum success. If you are trying to draw a new play in the dirt every month for your advertising, there is no way you can ever get ahead of everything that needs to be done. This is not a weekly or monthly commitment, but one for the entire year – and that brings me to the Five Reason Why You Plan Annually.

SEE THE BIG PICTURE.

The main element required going into an annual planning session is a 12-month calendar for the upcoming year so you can identify opportunities. These opportunities include:

- Months containing five Saturdays
- Paydays on the 1st and 15th
- Day of the week the holidays fall on; for example, July 4th on a Wednesday could be considered for an event
- Date of the last weekend of the month
- Number of days between December 25th and the following weekend (the earlier it falls in the week gives you a longer run at the weekend)
- Local school calendar (first and last day of the school year, Fall, Christmas and Spring Break)
- Dates of community events that tie up the market, such as music festivals or big games
- Dates a full moon appears because you better believe it has a positive effect on shoppers

Every year is different, but the one thing they all have in common is 365 days and 52 weeks. That will never change. Every month of every year is loaded for prime-time sales and service gains; you just have to map them out.

BUILD A PLAN BASED ON THE TOTAL HISTORY OF YOUR DEALERSHIP.

Once you have the next-year calendar marked for opportunistic marketing, base your plan on the total history of your dealership. To do this you will need access to previous budgets and sale records to be precisely aware of the seasonality and fluctuation that is inherent to your particular market. It is obvious that every market has unique quirks, some as obvious as, "This is when the weather makes an event questionable," to, "This month is when cold weather hits and the folks with money head south." The proper allocation of marketing dollars cannot be a snap judgment; precision planning is most effective when there is no other pressing deadline. Study the trends of your dealership against the rest of the market to see when you may have the best opportunity to gain market share.

BUY YOUR MEDIA AHEAD OF THE MARKET.

Media buying delivers the best ROI when you negotiate and purchase at a time when there are fewer competitors ready to pull the trigger. There is not much more that can be said other than this truly allows you to have the best rates. When you are the first to make buys and place orders you have the power of leverage on your side because vendors want to have money on the books. They want to be able to tell other dealers, "The competition has already placed an annual buy." You are in front of the media reps with bread in your hand at a time when they are starving for business, and historically more willing and eager to negotiate – that is a fact!

PLAN IN PLACE; CONFIDENCE IS HIGH.

I am going to quote an outside authority on this point because the cartoon character G.I. Joe said it best: "Knowing is half the battle!" From the owner to the managers to the advertising agency to the local media vendors, their confidence is high when a plan is in place that clearly reflects the best interests of the dealership. It erases uncertainty about what may be looming ahead when your team sees you making a proactive commitment. You will see a better ROI when everyone is pulling in the same direction to achieve the highest level of execution. Your marketing investment is too significant to even give breath to anyone employed saying, "Nobody told me we were having a sale." When you have top-to-bottom buy-in with everyone on the same page, expect great things to happen and build on it. This is why reviewing the previous year is such a key component because if a sale worked once, confidence should be so high that you can match that success or exceed it.

MORE TIME TO FOCUS ON MERCHANDISING AND EXECUTION.

The difference between the sky falling and the plan working is priceless. Are there going to be adjustments? Absolutely, because of factors that are beyond our control such as a tsunami, manufacturer recall, or government bailout. For sure there are no guarantees. The annual plan requires review. For some it is monthly but at least should be reviewed quarterly. The upside is having the time for key decision-makers to evaluate, modify and fine-tune to keep it rolling down that track.

You create the plan and you work the plan. That's execution and I think it is best symbolized by the famous line from an ex-NFL coach, "You play the game to win!" In every sport we have heard coaches comment during post-game interviews that they had the right play called with the right players in place but they did or didn't execute, and that was the difference between winning and losing the game. My favorite description of finishing in second place is the distinction of being "first loser" and that is all the incentive necessary to plan, to execute and to be better than anyone else.

In closing, the amount of time and effort you have put into connecting the dots of your annual plan should not be discounted at the first bump in the road. Your decisions have to be based on precedent when analyzing your market historically. Your execution has to be directed to where your market is at the present time, and with due diligence you will be up to speed on where the market is moving forward. We often think of the Internet boom as an almost overnight phenomenon. But in actuality the first link between computers was in 1969, the first webpage in 1991, the first smartphone in 1992 and Google's start-up was 1998. What is the next dot to be added to your annual plan? Today, just as it has always been in the continued pursuit of success, you need to be relentless in staying ahead of the curve.

14

THE SMARTEST INTERNET GUY IN THE ROOM

E verybody in the modern automotive sales and marketing industry has met this person before. It could have been at a manufacturer meeting, a dealer 20 group, an Internet training seminar, or even somebody that you have on staff or hired to train your people about Internet processes and executions. I have met this person many times in many different dealerships and settings, and each time I meet one of them they solidify certain characteristics. It almost seems like a cloning process where more and more of the same exact person shows up in different locations. This person should be called The Smartest Internet Guy in the Room for the obvious reason: They feel they know more about the tools to properly market through the Internet than anyone else has in history. When you hold the title of The Smartest Internet Guy in the Room, you like to talk about a lot of different applications and acronyms that go over most owners' and operators' heads. Not everyone with these qualities is a bad person or not knowledgeable, but I have run across a few that couldn't sell their way out of a wet paper bag. Most of them have very little retail experience but a lot of technical experience and that is what has landed them the position in the first place.

The fact of the matter is this person generally tries to act superior to all parties involved including dealership owners, general managers, advertising partners and anyone who has a question or new idea regarding e-commerce. The Smartest Internet Guy in the Room will generally argue a point by showing examples and using acronyms that nobody else understands so they can finally win a discussion and appear to have all the answers. Sometimes this person can even make dealers, factory people and other staff members actually think that he/she is an Internet wizard because nobody else understands.

The digital director of our company and I were recently in a dealership meeting where the Smartest Guy showed up and told us and the dealer everything that the factory recommended the dealer should be doing in regards to his store's digital marketing. After watching the ideas and acronyms fly back and forth for about two hours, I asked the dealer if he wanted to step outside and grab a cup of coffee. Once we left the conference room he asked me, "What in the world are they talking about?" (This is a dealer in his 50s who is moderately progressive but is no self-proclaimed Internet guru.) I told him that the factory guy was trying to prove to everyone in the meeting that he was The Smartest Internet Guy in the Room. The dealer laughed, "Just do what you need to in order to get us the most for our money and the best source of traffic."

After witnessing this event multiple times in multiple stores, I decided to write about how to understand the voodoo of Internet terminology. There is a foundational philosophy that I believe in when it comes to executing and marketing your dealership on the Internet. Too many dealers have told me they know very little about the Internet. And how many of them truly know much about the elements of traditional media? Everyone has been exposed to it and knows the acronyms of TRP (target rating point), GRP (gross rating point) and CPP (cost per point), but how many dealers know the formula to calculate reach and frequency? If I asked 10 dealers today how to calculate a GRP, I bet only a couple could accurately tell me how to get to the number and what it truly means. I'm not trying to be negative towards any dealer, but that's why you use vendors and companies who know what these things mean. Most owners and operators have spent millions of their own and the factory's dollars on traditional media, but truly knowing all the inner workings of traditional media can be just as confusing to them as these Internet phrases and acronyms.

Internet marketing should be treated no differently than traditional marketing. Owners may feel lost when it comes to how they should deal with Internet marketing because it is ever changing and so vast. My advice is for you to assemble a team of both internal dealership personnel and outside vendors to accomplish your goal of more traffic. This, in turn, results in more opportunities followed by more sales and lets your team get down to business and go to work. That may sound too simple but I have seen it work in many dealerships for many years now and it doesn't take a rocket scientist to execute.

You have to pick the areas on the Web that are going to get the most impressions and direct traffic to your website or one of your virtual properties. Then you have to stick to your plan and execute. People who want to spout different theories and ideas with no practical way to execute will never go down in history as great marketers or great retailers. They will always be known as "the guys who talked too much." They'll also lose the battle for the title of The Smartest Internet Guy in the Room. So when they come into your dealership or try to sell you something by telling you what you are doing wrong, take it with a grain of salt. Find the right people to create a plan and then stick to your plan until you have found the ceiling (which is never, by the way).

The following are definitions and descriptions of the most popular words and practices that will be thrown around in today's dealership environment. It is okay if you haven't heard all of them before, but use this guide to educate yourself so you understand what to look for should one of these Internet gurus try to talk you or a member of your organization in circles.

DEFINITIONS & DESCRIPTIONS:

Search Engine Marketing (SEM): an umbrella term for online advertising and website promotion. Related synonyms include SEO, PPC, email marketing, paid inclusion, behavioral targeting, and retargeting. SEM can either be all or part of these different components but this is the most prevalent term used in our industry today.

Search Engine Optimization (SEO): the onsite tactics for increasing the potential for high rankings in the natural search (i.e. organic) results for specific keywords. How well a website is optimized determines how high you are going to appear in the list and how many different times you appear in search results.

Search Engine Algorithm: a set of rules used to rank the listings contained within its index relating to an exact keyword query. SE algorithms are black boxes. No one knows exactly how their algorithms function, as protection from competitors and those who wish to spam. That said, by observation and experience, there are fairly well known guidelines of how the algorithms work.

Index: the collection of information a search engine has that searchers can query against. With crawler-based search engines, the index is typically copies of all the web pages they have found from searching the Web.

Search Engine Ranking Placement (SERP): This cannot be purchased in natural search results (meaning you can't pay Google to be number one on the right-hand side of Google results). The site must contain information that is relevant to create a high rank.

Pay-Per-Click (PPC): a type of paid Internet advertising where the advertiser pays only when the ad is clicked on. PPC's advantage over other ad types is that PPC ads (text or images) are displayed based on a trigger. Most often this is a user's search query (the search engine will match it with a proprietary relevant algorithm), though they are also displayed on some webpages based on that page's theme. The relevant keywords are purchased by advertisers, often via an auction like Google AdWords. These text or image ads are subsequently distributed by the search engines over their affiliated system of websites.

AdWords: Google's proprietary ad serving system.

Cost-Per-Click (CPC):   the metric that divides advertising spending by the number of clicks. This is one way, but not necessarily the best or only way, to determine if a campaign is effective. This is something most Internet search companies brag about, but it's not the only way to measure effectiveness.

Click-through Rate (CTR): the ratio that shows the number of people who saw your ad and clicked it. Divide the number of impressions of any type of digital ad received by the number of people who clicked the ad and went to the website. Text ads, graphic ads, and targeting ads will all have different rates of what is average and acceptable.

Cost-Per-Lead (CPL): a method of paying for macro conversion (a qualified lead through a site) instead of an intermediary action (visitors or clicks). This is the ultimate measurement of how much money was spent versus how many leads were generated.

Cost-Per-Acquisition (CPA): the cost of acquiring one customer; one of the ultimate return-on-investment (ROI) calculations.

Cost-Per-Thousand (CPM): the cost per thousand impressions (M being the Roman numeric symbol for thousand). CPM is a traditional media term for measuring number of impressions. It's typically used in branding campaigns.

Behavioral Targeting (BT): based on data profiles created during a consumer's visit to a website (type of site, pages visited, time on page, links clicked, etc.). The profile is attached to the user's browser and as a result, site publishers can use this data to create defined audience segments based on visitors that have similar profiles. When visitors return to a specific site or a network of sites using the same web browser, those profiles can be used to allow advertisers to position their online ads in front of those visitors who exhibit a greater level of interest and intent for the products and services being offered.

Retargeting (RT): the use of a site visitor's search history as a basis for the ads that the visitor will see. Graphic ads of various sizes will follow a user around while they are on various websites and serve ads up for a dealership's site that you have visited.

Keywords: single words or multi-word phrases that are used in a search engine query. In the context of SEO, the most popular keywords are selected (based on historical search data) for the best organic search and PPC performance. Keyword research is the indispensable foundation of SEO for web pages and PPC ads.

Quality Score: an estimate of how relevant your ads, keywords, and landing page are to a person seeing your ad. Your quality score can affect ad position and CPC.

Long Tail Search: the vast number of low-volume, high-quality transactional search phrases (i.e. 2007 white Toyota Camry LE with red leather). While individually there are not a lot of search terms exactly like this, there are, cumulatively, an extremely large number of variations. The automotive long tail in particular can almost be infinite.

Organic Traffic: traffic that came to your site from an organic listing on a search engine. No money was spent to generate this traffic it just found you by searching.

Organic Listing: Also referred to as a natural listing, these are search page results that are free and based upon the search algorithms of that particular search engine.

Referral Traffic: a measure of the visitors that get to your site via a link from another site.

Referral Domain: the website address from which referral traffic came to your site.

Direct Traffic: someone who went to a search engine or Internet browser and typed in your exact URL web address.

Live Chat: a box or button where website visitors can type in a question and get an immediate answer. This is a lot like sending text messages on a cell phone. It doesn't require sending an email and is immediate.

Click to Call: a button or icon on a site where the visitor can place a phone call to the dealership directly from the website. This tool is most commonly used on and applicable to mobile-site technology.

Conversions: a specific action related to a user's behavior and engagement that are tracked and measured. There are two types of conversions that are most widely evaluated. Typical conversions include:

Macro Conversions

- Email leads
- Request for more information
- Phone calls from the website
- Request for Information (RFI)
- Sales
- Chat

Micro Conversions

- Product or service PDFs downloaded
- Contact page visited
- Map page visited
- Directions page visited
- Submit lead page visited
- Videos watched

Conversion Optimization :the use of analytics and test variations in page design and messaging in an effort to maximize the conversion ratio. Or, the number of website visitors who become paying customers. This is particularly important for e-commerce sites and sites with higher traffic levels.

Link Building: typically identifies, qualifies, and then pursues the best link opportunities in your industry. This may include free, paid or reciprocal links.

Now you have what I call "the buzzword list," but don't stop here. Talk to your people both internally and externally and show them this list and make sure they understand what these words mean to your traffic, your sales and their paychecks. Embrace what is being discovered with how you can market and be effective on the Internet. It's continuing to become a larger percentage of your business with every passing minute. More people are using it today than ever and a properly crafted Internet marketing plan does not cost nearly the investment that a similar plan in traditional media will cost.

You have to get on track right now to stay ahead of the curve as this road unfolds. There is an old saying, "One of these days is none of these days," and the Internet waits for no one. Even without being the Smartest Internet Guy in the Room, there is no doubt in my mind that the Internet has the power to generate traffic in numbers we will marvel at one day.

15

THE PERFECT STORM OF TRAFFIC

There are a lot of dealers and automotive marketers that currently struggle with how to spend their advertising dollars. Everywhere you look, somebody has an opinion as to how you should allocate marketing dollars between traditional media and digital media. The statistics and numbers of what should be spent and where vary depending on who you ask, but oftentimes when you get into one of these discussions, the word you do not hear enough is traffic.

People get so wrapped up in the smaller digital details of clicks, impressions, conversions, optimization and video while forgetting the big picture. A finely tuned marketing plan will build momentum and generate traffic. In this plan, every penny spent to promote a dealership, whether to the general market or through digital media, is the dealership's investment in traffic. The investment will either over-deliver (which is the sign of an incredibly efficient plan) or under-deliver (dollars are spent on wasted forms of advertising). Since most owners and operators are big-picture thinkers and leave the details and executions to the people they have put in place, I want to break this traditional/digital discussion down from a big-picture point of view. What follows is an explanation of how traditional and digital media must truly complement each other and be used in tandem to grow your traffic every day. I call this seven-step process "The Perfect Storm of Traffic" to illustrate how each piece must be present to create the largest waves of customers in the dealership.

The constant battle in today's dealership marketing plan is making people realize that both types of media, whether traditional or digital, are ultimately going to lead 80 to 90 percent of traffic to your website first before they ever set foot inside the dealership. In fact, the average dealership that our company worked with in 2012 got 20 times more visitors to their website than the number that physically visited their dealership. But just like walking on a stairway, if you miss one step, you can take a serious tumble.

STEP 1

Traditional advertising messages run through wide-reaching outlets, including broadcast and satellite television, radio, satellite radio, cable or a similar platform, newspaper, direct mail, outdoor, and point-of-sale materials. These advertisements build dealership awareness with the general public and give your dealership mental shelf-space for consideration when someone enters the shopping funnel. Both your market and your budget will dictate which ones you target, but my recommendation is to always pick the one that can reach the most intenders for your product the most times and with the greatest frequency. Every DMA (Designated Market Area) has different cost structures that will impact the type of media you want to run to the general market. Every dealership has its own unique message that can also influence what type of media is best. I repeat: The bottom line is to select the one type of outlet that will reach the most intenders for your product the most times with the greatest frequency.

Once you have selected and placed your media, your advertising message must remain consistent in its style so it builds a lasting impression over time. Because you have chosen far-reaching media outlets, you are creating big, booming impressions with a large amount of people for a long period of time. In these messages, you must make sure to present and promote the dealership's web address in repetitious ways so that the consumer is over-exposed to your online presence. Sell the dealership, sell the deal and sell the place online or in the store, all while knowing that eight to nine out of 10 people will go to the website first. You are obligated to address both physical location and virtual location. This is why I preach to dealers that to sustain mental shelf-space in the mind of the consumer you must stay consistent week after week and month after month with the right message through the right media. You must establish connectivity that results in your market thinking of you first. The on-going quality of execution drives your dealership to be top-of-mind and the payoff is proven because people generally look to those who are the biggest advertisers first when they start their shopping process.

STEP 2

Your initial consistency in reaching a mass market will pay off when people enter the buying cycle. Instead of a new shopper going online and visiting manufacturer or third-party sites, they will start the process by searching for your dealership directly. This is a huge advantage because we know for a fact that 80 to 90 percent will begin by looking at your website, doing research and narrowing down their selection process. The consumer today has shown they will go online to learn about vehicles they are interested in buying. They will attempt to evaluate the value of their current trade-in, but it is a magical thing when they start this process on your site rather than going anywhere else to look.

If the ads in Step 1 have been successful in building top-of-mind awareness in shoppers, whether they have ever done business with your dealership or not, you will have a shot at them because they will go online and begin searching for you. The ultimate goal of tier three creative in our company is to sell the deal, the dealership and the URL. This allows the dealership to have a higher percentage of direct and referral traffic. The more effective and creative the media, the more people will be looking directly for you online. This totally dismantles the traditional purchase funnel model that I believe in and actively use, but again that is why this model is called the "The Perfect Storm of Traffic." It is rare to see but you can control the customer better when they start with you, and at that point the game is yours to lose.

STEP 3

It would literally take a blank check written for unlimited advertising every month to insure that every person who enters the purchase funnel goes online looking directly for you. Even though it appears that this would be great, there are still so many other dealers aggressively promoting to the same audience that you would never be able to achieve a 100 percent capture rate of your audience. Once that customer is searching and shopping online, you must have the digital executions in place to turn online shoppers into unique visitors to your site. Step 3 compiles all the pieces that you are using to snag more online searchers and drives them to your site before they go to someone else's.

These Internet customers looking at dealers/manufacturers and trade-in evaluation sites are known as low-hanging fruit. These are buyers who are looking to buy something today, and if not today, then their ideal purchase date is not very far into the future. Hopefully these buyers were exposed to your dealership message in Step 1, but somehow you were not their first shopping choice in Step 2 and now they are out there with the rest of the pack. This is where efforts regarding search engine marketing and search engine optimization come into play. The easier your website is to find by all search engines, the more impressions you are going to make, which mathematically equates to more people visiting on your site. This is why it is critical that you have a well-balanced plan so your dollars can be spent to maximize online exposure. When shoppers are online and cannot find you, you have no chance with them. Just because you have a new car franchise in an assigned market area doesn't mean that everyone will find you or even know that you exist. Whatever funnel theory you subscribe to, it is clear most shoppers do not pay attention to dealers or their ads until they are in the market to buy. And when they are, you better have every digital trigger in place to be in their face and get as much traffic as you can stand.

STEP 4

Now that a person has either gone online to shop from you directly, as in Step 2, or found you through your digital marketing efforts in Step 3, the bottom line is they have found you. And now what do you do with them? Step 4 is all about one thing—your website. The website is your virtual dealership, and as mentioned earlier, it will probably get 20 times more traffic than your physical dealership. But that number is only going to increase in the future. I have been exposed to and worked with all existing major website providers and platforms and I think the technology available to dealers through these companies offers endless possibilities to what you can do with your virtual space. Are some site providers better than others? Sure they are. I don't have a preference because there are strengths and weaknesses with them just like there are with anything else. Your challenge is to first pick the best website provider that is right for your dealership and your new car franchise and then set up a plan for how to make your site superior to your competition's website.

A shopper is going to look at many things when they are searching for a new or used vehicle on your site. The first thing they are look- ing at is inventory and pricing. If these two things are hard to find, you are not going to retain much of the traffic you have worked so hard to create. Customers are always looking for deals and specials. Making these key attractions easy to find and highlighted will help garner more interest from the traffic, and common sense must apply. Vehicles in the most popular color need to be the ones presented in special graphics and the same goes for information posted to the site because those are the colors that the masses will be buying. When it comes to used cars, you have to have a laundry list of all the features and benefits that the vehicle has to offer. No two used cars are alike. I'm preaching loudly here, but price is going to be the number one driver of used car leads once traffic is on the site. Finance information, trade-in evaluation tools and credit applications are a must. Even though their use is going to be less than what you probably imagine, they still must be prevalent and easy to navigate.

Finally, your site must look alive. The presentation needs to look exciting and inviting. Take some time to study websites of major retailers like Target and Best Buy and notice how they showcase products and specials in a very creative and colorful way. Nothing says that a dealer's site has to look plain and desolate with dark color schemes. Create and manage your site. Be a window into your dealership, reflecting a look and content relevant to your marketing message. Across the board dealers pay far too little attention to the upkeep of their site and its content. Think about all the money spent to landscape, cut the grass, clean the windows of the dealership on a monthly basis and then think about what you spend to keep your website looking exciting. I know the difference is probably shocking, especially considering which one gets 20 times more traffic than the other.

STEP 5

The next challenge you have to address is Step 5, the "Zero Moment of Truth." This is the very instance when an online shopper progresses to an "up" by sending in an email lead, starting a live chat, or calling the dealership directly. Step 5 is the precise second when the online shopper reaches out to you much in the same way a physical "up" turns into your lot, parks their car, and gets out to shop. In both cases it is a time of first impressions. You only get one chance to make them. When the online customer sends out the request for information on a vehicle, you must have a perfect plan in place with the right people lined up ready to respond with proper information in a lightening-fast manner.

There's no question that in the last few years the amount of sales-related phone calls has declined rapidly as more people choose to send in an email instead of enduring the painful process of dialing a dealership and trying to talk to a salesperson. But clicks or calls, this step is critical because this one pivotal moment is where all the effort is going to pay off with either a victory or a defeat. Think of Step 5 just like a college football team who has trained and practiced week after week to be prepared and now is on the field for the season opening kickoff. It's the same as when a customer presses *send* for an email or a cell phone call, the game is on. That inquiry is flying through the air and you either catch it and run with it or get tackled by the other team. You're the head coach, ultimately responsible for having your team ready in Step 5 to win favor from the opening whistle—the alternative is not an option. You can bet that you are probably not the only dealership that a customer is shopping, so even though you are starting out on a level playing field with your competition, how you respond and what you respond with is either going to put you on the shopping list or take you off in a very short time. Dealerships and customer retention tools are loaded with automatic responders and canned replies, which are okay for the very first thing that gets sent back, but then the question comes, "What do we do next?"

STEP 6

It's time to separate the men from the boys. Step 6 is when and how the personal execution of your Internet department or business development becomes a game changer. Effectively working the systems and processes that you use, your team is either going to help you turn the lead into a live customer on your showroom floor or send them knocking on another dealer's door. The more professional and personable they are, the quicker their responses. Your team's ability to provide instant and accurate information will win over more customers. I wrote about this earlier. Based on responses and follow-up for the new car side, you must have an aggressively priced vehicle, and on the used car side, vehicles that are priced according to the market. Step 6 is truly where you begin to close the deal with your online customer because the more responses and follow-ups that are sent, the more the customer starts buying the salesperson/dealership just as much as they are buying the car. Think about the traditional 12-step "Road to the Sale," where the salespeople are taught to build rapport with the in-store customer. The only difference with the online shopper is the salespeople are building rapport and trust through email dialogue and phone calls. And the dealer who wins Step 6 is the one who is the best with online follow-up, customer treatment, and most importantly, pricing to transform the online "up" into a physical "up" standing on the lot to see the vehicle they are interested in purchasing.

STEP 7

The final step in our journey is what I call "You Had Me at Hello." It's all you can ask for as a destination! It comes when the shopper who is satisfied with their research gets together with your people who worked the dealership's processes to perfection and everyone meets at their vehicle of interest for a firsthand look. And unless something is very wrong with the situation, this is a true "you had me at hello" moment because this shopper should be leaving your dealership as a buyer in the vehicle they wanted. There will always be customers who don't buy because the car just isn't right for them or they assumed they could get a little more for their trade. But more often than not at this point in the process, you should generally be dealing with truly qualified and serious shoppers whose intent is to buy from your dealership. It is both an amazing and arduous process when you think about it. The customer started out and either searched for you directly or found you through searching. Then your website was more appealing which caused them to look until they found exactly what they wanted. Next, your people and processes took over and turned this shopper into a buyer. Unless there is something wrong—and there can be hiccups, like the car in person wasn't what they wanted, it had flaws or an issue with price or trade value—this should be the easiest deal of all!

Still, once the customer arrives at the dealership, nothing should be taken for granted. You should carry out the scenario that you see worked every day. The customer is shown the vehicle and all the features and benefits in person. Next is the test drive to insure to the customer this vehicle is exactly what they want and deliver peace of mind. Then the customer sits down with a salesperson or manager to review all the numbers and the deal is either settled or the customer has to go home and think about it. Done deal or not, the customer should then be shown the entire dealership and given all standard reasons to buy from you as practiced with all customers. And finally, you have either sold a vehicle or given someone a solid case to buy it from you and buy it today.

Obviously nobody closes 100% of their customers, but when you take yourself through these steps and think through the process from a big-picture perspective, the only real reason someone shouldn't be buying is because the final car isn't right for them, or financially it wasn't feasible. Unfortunately, you will always have some unreasonable people, but this process is a sound way to follow and direct the customer's migration south to the very bottom of the purchase funnel.

"The Perfect Storm for Traffic" paints a picture of how the marriage of both dimensions—traditional marketing dollars and digital marketing dollars—should be used to create and propel this buying cycle. The seven-step principles are very close foundationally to what is laid out in the first chapter where we defined the three types of traffic: customers who are going to find you naturally, those who find you through your ads and then your current customer base, who is going to be looking for you and only you. Customers are going to come to you in a thousand different ways from a thousand different online sources. So in truth, you will probably never be able to determine which single digital tool led a customer to you, especially because that number is only going to grow with each passing month and year. The dealers who outpace the market and are the more forward-thinking of automotive retailing are the ones who plan, visualize and execute the perfect balance between both dimensions of the media to produce next day traffic…and never miss a step!

16

PRICE AND ONLINE MERCHANDISE

s the Internet has evolved into the most widely used source for vehicle shopping, the habits and practices that dealers use to sell cars over the Internet has changed with it. It is not a question of whether you have a website or not, but a question of how many *different* sites you have. Some dealers who have only one franchise are branching out to have separate websites for new cars, used cars, finance and even service. It's not a matter of having an Internet manager in your dealership, but the amount of people who are in your Internet department. And it's not about how much you spend on advertising dollars to drive digital traffic, but the amount of your digital spend relative to the amount of traffic you get. There are definitely a lot of questions, some that were being talked about five to 10 years ago, that are now a fact and no longer require discussion.

One such question is whether or not you price your vehicles on the Internet. Many dealers as recently as five years ago were still pondering this notion: Can you get away with putting your cars online without a price? It was a hot topic, and in meetings as well as general discussions I had with owners and general managers, they were always looking for angles to hold more gross per copy. Just as the way you use the Internet has changed, pricing has changed with it. Let me be very clear: If you are not putting prices on every piece of your online inventory then you are leading to your own digital demise. Online pricing is the determining factor in how many of your online viewers becomes in-store shoppers. If there are no prices— *aggressive* prices—then all the views that you are getting on your website will simply seek out other dealers online who do have prices posted.

American consumers have been trained, through their use of the Internet, to search for the item they want with the lowest price they can get. It is no secret why it is done—they want the best deal and do not really care where it comes from as long as it is the merchandise that they want. Take the now-famous Monday after Thanksgiving, "Cyber Monday," for instance. The biggest draw among a poll of Internet shoppers who said they shopped online this day was that most major retailers offered free shipping. The news media makes it out to be a day when people are still searching and looking for deals they might have missed over the weekend, but that is not accurate. The public has found that they can save money on shipping charges, which has become a major hook used by most retailers on Cyber Monday, and shoppers factor this in when evaluating the best deal. No consumer ever wants to pay too much for something, so they use the Internet to aggressively research before making a retail purchase.

Vehicles have to be handled the same way. There are two points that sum up the entire evolution of the Internet as it relates to today's car shopper: 1) They are looking for the prefect vehicle. 2) They want to know what it costs. It's just that simple—information and price. People will use other tools like trade-in evaluators or credit applications online, but when the rubber meets the road, it comes down to the right car and right price.

Here are the six points that you must make sure are covered because the right car at the right price is so critically important.

1) Prices Sell New Cars

Shoppers are going to do their homework to narrow down the list of cars that they want. By the time the masses are on your site they already know which car with what options and usually have a short list of colors that they prefer. This is why new car pricing is so critical and must both be posted and be aggressive. If you are in a more crowded metro market then you probably already know the drill. You have to be as aggressive, if not more aggressive, than your competitors, or else the customer is not going to come to you. Even if you have fewer dealers in your market, you probably still debate how aggressive you need to be with pricing. Don't get fooled into thinking that you can let up and not aggressively price your cars, and don't mistake that by aggressive pricing I mean every car has to be a "loss leader." Yes, your advertised specials will usually be aggressive but the rest of the inventory can be priced according to what you see as the market price as well as what buyers would pay for these cars. The real secret to how you turn more views on your website into customers on the showroom floor is to develop and maintain an aggressive pricing strategy for your website. You can't hide the price of the car or pretend that you don't know the price of the car. The customer is only interested in your car if they know what it is going to cost them.

2) Price and Descriptions Sell Used Cars

It has been said that "no two used cars are identical." Where two used cars are listed side by side on the Internet, that statement is more true than ever. Pricing on used is still going to be the greatest motivator but following close behind and justifying the price are the details. As people also say, "The devil is in the details." That is especially the case with used cars. Great descriptions for each used car in your digital inventory will do the job of acting as a virtual salesman for the dealership. If the details and descriptions sell the car as the very best possible car for the person who reads it, then you are going to engage more of these shoppers and turn them into leads.

The details on new vehicles are generally taken care of with your website provider or through your Original Equipment Manufacturer (OEM), but there is nobody who will do this for you with your used cars…except you. All the car's features should be included, with a key emphasis on the bells and whistles. Each description should tell a story about the car and its history. Did the car have one owner? Does it have low mileage? Does it appear to have been garage-kept? Is the interior plush and looking just like it did when it was sitting in the showroom? Remember, you see these cars everyday but the person shopping from their computer or phone is seeing this car for the first time and only if it impresses them enough will they become more interested. This isn't easy work to do. It needs to be done for every used car on your lot, but the reward in the amount of your next day traffic who becomes *next day buyers* will be well worth it.

3) Great Pictures

You can no longer have only a couple of pictures of each car and believe that you are satisfying today's shopper. You need somewhere between 24 to 36 pictures of each car that you have listed! Notice that I said *each* car. That means *every* new and used car. Many dealers rely on the manufacturer to frame in or host their new car inventory, which is fine, but you need additional pictures of all the cars, and again I emphasize not just your used cars. It is a simple process and one that is critical in giving the shopper a reason to get more excited about the vehicle. Also, these pictures need to be shot in a controlled/planned setting. They cannot just be shot somewhere along the side of a building showing asphalt. There are dealers today building "shooting rooms" or finding places in their dealerships to set up so every car can be shot with the same background. The only thing that changes in each picture is the car. Having great pictures and a great place to shoot them is a trend that started a few years ago. All dealers are going to have to embrace this trend or be left behind. Today's shoppers want to see the car from all interior and exterior angles to see if it truly is the car for them.

4) Video

Just as all of the cars need actual photos, the cars need videos as well. If you have a setting where you can take pristine pictures of cars, I suggest that you use the same area to shoot short, easy-to-upload videos that customers can view as well. Dealers who have started using real videos on their cars are finding that their web leads and conversion from online traffic have steadily increased. Whether it is a new car or a used car, videos allow you to narrate a story and point out features and benefits exclusive to the exact vehicle. Creating and loading videos into online descriptions allows for longer engagement with the shopper. It creates the opportunity to point out something that the shopper would otherwise not have seen or known about the car. Plus, you have something unique especially for your used cars that allow you to show and tell that story about why this car is so special. The final point is that the more videos that you have on your website, the better you are optimizing your website. Videos will help you drive up your organic search results as well as allow you to create a very large presence for your dealership on YouTube, which aids in optimization efforts.

5) Virtual Sales Pitch

This could also be called the reason to buy from you, but the term "virtual sales pitch" sounds a whole lot cooler and is a vital part of what you are selling to the shopper. (This isn't a typical item so follow closely as the virtual sales pitch is described in order to develop one if it doesn't already exist for your dealership.) Every car on your lot that is listed on your website should have an expressed reason to buy from your dealership. The reason can be anything at all but it must be there so people can read it, and even after they have decided on the price and vehicle, it will reinforce your dealership. You may be known as a good place to do business. You may be an award-winning dealership. You may offer a special after-market warranty package or program that has great advantages to the customer. It can be any of these things as long as it is there. People do not trust car dealerships—that has not changed and, in my opinion, it will never change—so anything that you can do to overcome objections must be done at all steps of the buying process. Because the salesperson isn't there to talk to them when they are looking online, you have to make this present in your vehicle descriptions. Again it has to be on every item. The virtual sales pitch will help you after people have settled on a car and a price that makes them feel comfortable.

6) Vehicle History Report

This is where CARFAX is the king for your used-vehicle inventory. There are other services out there that ultimately do the same thing, but CARFAX has done a great job of branding their company to the public. They have become a household name, like FedEx, Coca-Cola and Xerox. People want to know the history of a used car and with these tools available, why would you consider not showing them the information? Information is crucial to the Internet shoppers, so give it to them before they have to ask for it! Shoppers are going to want to see the vehicle history report, especially if that car is high on their consideration list. Plus, the older the car with more miles, the more valuable this is going to be for the person looking at the car. The costs are minimal and they should be posted to every used car on your site as well as be easy to find. If you have a customer who has not bought a used car before and has not heard of CARFAX or other vehicle-history report companies, then this is just another tool you have in your arsenal that will help gain their trust and bring them closer to buying from you. If you are not using a source for vehicle-history reports then start immediately; if you are not using CARFAX you need to consider changing to them immediately.

These critical elements must be present in your price and online merchandise strategy. More things will evolve as time goes by and you will have to adapt to them, but in order to convert your next-day traffic into next day buyers, you are going to have to make everything easy for them while presenting exactly what they want. No, an aggressive online pricing structure isn't the best way to generate gross and there are ways around it that you can find within your own dealership. But yes, this strategy is the best way to sell more new and used cars out of the traffic that you are already getting. If you are the dealership that wants to get ahead and grow at a more rapid pace than the competition, you will have to embrace these six elements and use them to your full advantage.

17

BUYING SPONSORSHIP VERSUS BUYING LEVERAGE

The following chapter is brought to you in part by…no one! Why? Because there is no real advantage to driving next day traffic by sponsoring something that attracts the interest of only a specific few. This chapter is dedicated to the discussion of the return on investment of money spent buying sponsorships versus buying leverage. After thinking about how many times a year I am asked to analyze different sponsorships, it became obvious that there are dos and don'ts on this subject that must be addressed. Before diving into the details, remember that most of the time sponsorships and advertising packages are nothing more than a bundle of very high-perceived value. They intend to make the package look more attractive by saddling it with a lot of worthless parts that dilute ROI. When you are responsible for making decisions that will generate traffic no matter what the dollar amount of your advertising budget or the size of your market, you are faced with the difficult process of unraveling a day-to-day dilemma. It is a risk/reward scenario because there are temptations that will cross your desk every day that may look and sound like a worthwhile venture, but at the end of the day, they are not efficient ways to advertise. This topic covers all facets of advertising and is not limited to any one particular item. If you have spent any time running a dealership or its marketing plan, you know that you'll have to make decisions on literally hundreds of these situations.

I understand this is a delicate question because of the position an automotive dealership has in the community. As a business owner, you have a responsibility to your local community to be a good supporter of all things local, but to yourself, your owner, or your employees, you have a responsibility to be fiscally conservative and provide a firm financial foundation for your business. Quite frankly, you have a target on your back as a source of monetary support for everything. Sponsorship opportunities arise from Little League Baseball and program ads for an art exhibit to media outlets selling you on the benefits of sponsoring the weather segment in the evening news for the third-ranked station in town. Because you are highly visible to the marketplace, both as a facility and an advertiser, they are going to come at you from all sides. When determining the best ways to drive next day traffic you are going to have to make the call regarding buying sponsorships or buying leverage.

Let me be clear on the difference between sponsorship requests that come from the community and those that are presented by the media. In terms of community involvement, I see more dealerships either earmark a budget amount or put a request-type system in place to handle appeals from civic-minded charities or organizations. These dollars come out of the business and are generally not charged to advertising and I agree with that thinking. In reality, your support of these ventures does not sell cars immediately. However, you are doing something that is of great worth to the community. Those involved with the cause will hold your dealership in high regard for your efforts and contribution. Even though there may be long-term benefits to charging these dollars to advertising, analyzing by a cost-per-car or a percent of gross is really difficult to justify. That is why more dealerships are moving toward making this a non-advertising related cost, so it doesn't skew the metrics and standards for tracking efficient advertising spending for their store.

Here is one final point in addressing who you support in the community. In the last two years I have seen more dealers move away from larger, more corporate charities like the Red Cross or United Way to more local, smaller-funded charities. This seems to resonate better within a hometown framework because it directly affects the lives and livelihoods of people working in the community. There have even been several dealerships that developed their own charities and created their own events to support the community, thus turning the tables and asking media vendors to support *our* cause rather than the other way around. This has been a winning scenario for the dealers bold enough to make the investments.

So now the question is media sponsorship versus media leverage in generating next day traffic and why it is so important. The answer is obviously the return on investment for the dollars that are being spent. It requires a significant portion of your operating budget every month to utilize the available tools to sell vehicles in volume in your community. The first thing that has to be addressed: By what standards do you define the most effective way of appropriating media dollars? Decisions must be based on the target audience and you must identify the media that is most efficient based on the budget dollars available. Note that this explanation has three distinct reference points: target audience, most efficient media, and available budget. (We are going to use the term "eye test" later in this chapter as the assessment you apply in determining the value of a sponsorship; each of these three points must be applied.)

One hundred percent of the goal in building a dealership's annual plan is to effectively apply the most dollars possible to media investments that efficiently influence your market. I can't say it enough and you can't lose sight of this guiding standard, especially when every media rep that calls on you will break out the smoke and mirrors to try and show you value in something that may truly be lacking. I tip my hat to their sales pitch because in a lot of cases many of these packages are loaded with what we call T-N-T: Tickets and Trips. This is one of the oldest, and still most popular, tricks in the book added to a package or sponsorship that is lacking in deliverables. Generally, if there are tickets or trips involved, raise a red flag immediately and begin to look for what may be hiding in the weeds. In addition to tickets and trips, when media outlets provide incentives that were contingent on the buy, buyer beware! You need to be on the lookout for why they feel the need to add incentives to make something attractive. In the words of our media director, "Buys can't be made just because the schedule is bundled with an added-value piece such as a trip; we buy all media based on its efficiency and if we end up qualifying for a trip based on that, then we will take part." Don't be blinded by emotion and put efficiency and effectiveness on the back burner, or you are getting ready to be roasted for your purchase.

Earlier in Chapter 13, we stated the biggest advantage of annual planning is your decision-making process. It's more effective without pressing deadlines or dealing with the smoke and mirrors that some vendors want to sell you on. The sponsorship or station package with a required level of spending may seem attractive, but when measured against the big-picture of efficiency and effectiveness, more often than not, it proves to be ineffective. Focus the budget dollars that you have on your target audience and the efficiency of your reach and let the reps go sell the package to the other dealers that are not as crafty in their thinking and planning as you have become.

I do not want to give the impression that you should slam the door on media reps, but rather, through the process of sorting the gems from the junk, you will be able to discern who truly wants to see your business do better through more traffic. Instead, you should scan what they are offering for the meat and evaluate if it fits into your current plans. Too many times, media outlets make a package conducive to their needs and not to the client's, and this is when you give it the "eye test" for efficiency and effectiveness.

If the offer is for a sponsorship consider if it is for a program segment, an event or an item that is popular in the market at the current time. For example, if it is late summer or early fall are they trying to sell you college or pro football? If it is a program segment then I generally stay away from it because our preference is to base buying decisions on previous performance and success. If adequate dollars are in the budget we should already be able to dominate this program segment with paid spots with an acceptable frequency—you do not need this offering. If the offer is to be part of a leading sponsor in a local event, here is where you check your heartstrings and personal likes at the door. Think about it from a logistical point of view and the size of the audience. It would be great to park cars and be a title sponsor of a local concert, but will your people actively work the event by not only taking cars out to the venue but actively engaging the crowd and searching for opportunity? And how big is the size of the audience that you will directly reach? Finally, if you are sponsoring something that is popular at the current time, does this offer give room for you to include your merchandising message as well as have your name mentioned and logo on screen?

If whatever is being offered by the media meets these criteria, then the next step is to counter the request. Your counteroffer could include any number of things such as narrowing the days in a group of spots or a shorter time frame to have more frequency. Use the tools of negotiating power—"Well, I will do it if you add this" or "That sounds good but what about including this?" The last and single greatest piece to work on if the package delivers is the cost—because nobody wants to pay retail prices, right?

If you have been involved in dealing with the media in your market, you know the playing field for media supremacy changes nearly as fast as the automotive industry. Every station is number one at something. Our agency fosters a belief in and has been fortunate over the years to build long-term relationships with our preferred media vendors. This has proven to be of clear advantage to our dealers. Our media vendors know we are not interested in packages or hot-commodity deals of the week so they know not to even bring them to us for review. We have found that the most successful thing that will generate traffic for a dealership is adding more to what is already there. We push for extra spots on top of what is already placed, and we reconcile and review all added value spots and require them to be logged and reported by the station in writing so we can see who is truly helping generate next day traffic. If a client has had a down month we can pick up the phone, explain the situation and request that our rep go in and add some extra spots to an existing buy. If the inventory is available, most reps are happy to help and boost the schedule because they have a fear of loss. If they don't go the extra mile, they may soon be losing precious dollars that are placed with them.

Does this relationship-building mentality sound familiar? I know you've said before that even though a customer didn't buy from you today, tomorrow is another day. Building relationships with media reps is going to reap benefits down the road, and that brings us to the discussion of legitimate sponsorships, added value and bonus spots. I have had many occasions when a rep who called my office gave me the first shot at a particular opportunity. Not junk or a bad package, mind you. But because they have come to value both our negotiating acumen and the depth of our relationship, they automatically think to include us first. Sometimes it is worthwhile and other times not, but it ultimately all comes down to the cost-per-point (CPP) that can be reached.

Sponsorships are evaluated with one strict standard. If it does not dilute or take away from monthly merchandising schedules, we take it as added value. When you nurture partnerships with media reps you utilize the most, you find that over time, they are willing to give away items that other clients have to purchase. Our company views being able to get "no charge" promotional pieces and sponsorships that cost your competition as leverage. This includes things such as sponsorships of local weather and/or Weather Channel banners. They may seem small, but they deliver a big audience when run consistently over time. They pass the "eye test," because people everywhere utilize weather sources in planning for their activities. This is just one small example but there are thousands of them out there that can be utilized for zero cost.

Added value can come in many different shapes and sizes. It is not all about getting free spots or a nice gift basket at Christmas. While writing this chapter I was reminded of one very important point regarding utilizing the media in the area of self-promotion. Our dealers have received news coverage when conducting events that benefit the community. (The event will often air on the 10 p.m. news as a feature story.) We have also received news media coverage when a special guest, such as a sports celebrity or business figure, made an appearance at the dealership. Added value comes in the form of media outlets coming on-site to report on what they perceive to be newsworthy events. This is probably the greatest public relations effort that a dealership can make—it is more readily accepted when delivered by a third party like a local media outlet and not as part of a paid advertisement from the dealership.

It goes without saying that when you request coverage for an event, in as few words as possible, don't forget to leverage the ad dollars you are spending to motivate these stations. If you give them ample time to assign crews, locate reporters and follow-up prior to your event, you stand a great chance of having your story make the local news and the impact of your event just went to a whole new level.

Bonus spots are the final piece to this formula because every station has extra inventory. Somewhere, somehow, they have unsold spots or schedules that get shuffled at the last minute when spots are moved or rearranged by advertisers. There are periods when stations will have more to give and periods when they will have less, but the bottom line is everybody has something that they can give you in terms of bonus spot weight. The golden rule of getting bonus spots is, "You will never get them unless you ask for them." Media reps who are going to be your true partners in delivering next-day traffic will find a way to deliver bonus spots to enhance your schedule. Make asking for and receiving bonus spots part of your ongoing media process and you will be amazed at what you are able to get.

Media dollars should not be spent for anything other than true market value. If a package, sponsorship, tickets or trips play a part in annual plan decision-making, you need to think again. The highest return on investment for each dollar spent on media is singular in its assessment. Does it drive traffic to your dealership? Hands down, the power of a leveraged media schedule promoting a big event far outweighs any sponsorship I have ever seen. I have not had one dealer tell me the response to their sponsorship of the community bulletin board was responsible for a successful month-end close, but I cannot begin to count the number of dealers who saw a Moonlight Madness Sale push their sales over forecast. The respect I have for dealers who support local charitable organizations is huge and without fail our dealers who develop their annual plan in anticipation of these needs are at the forefront. But do not allow your support of a charity to keep you from buying a media package as a gesture of goodwill. A lot of people think that buying tier three media is done by simply calling up a station and signing an order. If you believe that, then you will never be able to achieve the true value, efficiency and leverage that are possible from your investment in media.

18

GLORY DAYS

If you're in automotive advertising and you hear the phrase "let me tell you what we used to do that really worked," from a dealer or general manager, then you have one of two choices. You can sit there and listen to a story about the "glory days" of how they had the greatest marketing plan ever that brought in customers by the drove and everyone there made more money than U.S. Treasury prints in a year, or you can stop them before they ever start and ask, "If it worked so well then why did you ever stop doing it in the first place?"

Telling stories about the glory days occurs in many dealerships across the country and on a rather frequent basis. These stories are typically told by sales managers, used car managers, general managers, and every now and then, a dealer principal reflecting on how good things used to be back in the day. And there can be only one response to the glory-days crowd: "Why did you stop if it worked so well?" And nobody ever has a glorious answer for that. The truth of the matter is that things often didn't work as well as they are remembered and this is why dealerships got off that plan. We know the retail automotive sales business is full of excuses and reasons why things didn't happen as planned—the sale didn't work because it was a rainy day, a windy day, too hot, too cold, there was a football game on, or my all-time personal favorite, "The weather was perfect and nobody would be out buying a car on a day like that." The point is people in our business tend to exaggerate the reasons why things *do not* work in the same way they tend to exaggerate when they *do* work.

When it comes back around to making current advertising decisions, the inherent problem with exaggeration is that a lot of money is wasted based on what happened back in the glory days. When people talk your ear off about all the things that used to work so well, there is as much a component of bragging as there is encouragement for you to spend money on the type of advertising or promotion that they are talking about. I like to say over and over that everything is a function of the size of the market. "The bigger the sale, the greater the results," generally indicates that you had a great promotion and you caught the market at the right time. This same application applies when a sale is a failure because you could have the best creative, the best media and digital strategy, but if the market is not in the buying mode, then you are barking up the wrong tree.

Because I am a huge proponent of the philosophy "if it ain't broke then don't fix it," I find myself suspect of past silver-bullet scenarios that are out there in many dealerships today. To be effective with any kind of dealership marketing, as stated several times in previous chapters, you must remain consistent. If you do what I do for a living, you are going to hear a lot of stories about the glory days, but what I stand on is that there is a reason that things came to an end. My obligation is to stop clients from experimenting with advertising dollars that are meant to generate traffic based on what will drive traffic tomorrow, not five years ago.

I remember very vividly the first glory days moment that I encountered in a store a long time ago. My company had just picked up the dealership as a client because the previous agency had done a woeful job and lost market share through bad advertising and wasteful spending. In our initial marketing meeting, there was a whole team of managers in the room who wanted to tell me the same thing—the reason that the dealership wasn't selling any cars was because they were no longer using their once-famous jingle. I heard tales of how they sold 600 cars a month solely because of the jingle and how everybody in the market knew them because of this jingle. In my opinion, the jingle was memorable because it was so bad and hokey-sounding. But the real problem I had with it was the dealership name was sung only one time in the first nine seconds of the jingle and even that one time was hard to understand.

Did I argue the point right then? No. I did what any good marketer would do and set out to prove what I knew right from the start. I set up a local focus group. First, they heard the jingle without the words, only the music bed, and were polled to find out if they could recognize the jingle. To no surprise, over 70 percent of the focus group knew that they had heard it before and a handful started to sing along when they heard the music. Next, we played the jingle with all the singing and asked the group if they could tell us the name of the dealership. Only forty percent of the group could understand the name of the dealership that was being sung.

I would like to say everyone applauded my insight when I then took the findings back to the dealership and presented them to the owner and his managers. The findings showed that while 70 percent loved the jingle, only 40 percent knew that it was their dealership being promoted. It did not help that the name was sung too fast and the accent of the voiceover was not conducive to all languages that were present in the market. Even though this research had been conducted by a professional research firm, the managers still wanted to debate the fact that this jingle was their end-all salvation. Not one person with the dealership understood or appreciated the sample size of persons studied. And they had no comprehension that the statistical margin of error should have put the jingle on the shelf. All they knew was that they liked their jingle and wanted to hear it on the radio.

Fast-forward seven years. At the time I started handling their account, the dealership was one of four competing dealers in a metro market and holding 16.9 percent of the market in new car sales. Today they are holding 29.2 percent of the market and have had steady gains in both sales and profitability each year. The jingle was dropped on day one of the marketing plan that I instituted; the managers who wanted to run their old jingle didn't last 12 months working for the store. The owner reaffirmed his trust in our agency when he realized that his managers were more interested in dabbling with advertising than they were at desking and closing deals. As a result, he went out and found new people who were clear on working car deals and leaving the advertising up to the experts.

Another example of glory-days advertising practices occurred recently when a sales manager who was in his late 50s insisted that we should be mailing 30,000 to 40,000 pieces of mail in a month in order to generate traffic. He went on to say that he had grown a small-town import dealership to the highest volume and most profitable dealership of his brand in his region by doing mail back in the 1980s. And today mail was going to be the sole stimulus to the store's success. In his opinion, he didn't believe that the Internet sold cars or that TV, radio or email marketing generated any type of real traffic for a dealership—it was all done through mail and mail alone.

As evidence, this manager went on to talk about how he had run a sale that was so big that the police had to be called in for crowd control and parking because people were parking in the middle of the street to come shop. This guy had such a vivid memory of this sale held back in the 1980s that he had forgotten he was supposed to sell cars in the current month. His vision of the glory days had jaded his ability to operate in the present, and now the store was having one of its worst years ever at a time when the rest of the industry was picking up in volume.

This manager was totally baffled when I presented to his owner a plan that consisted of a very small amount of highly targeted owner-body mail with a heavy digital/email campaign directed at conquest buyers. It is amazing how a little bit of planning and insightful research can go such a long way into generating immediate traffic for a dealership. Within the next ninety days under a plan of less than 5,000 pieces of mail combined with a very aggressive digital presence, this store had once again regained its leadership in the market. This was a very simple plan that reached out to a select few previous customers of the dealership. The dominating online presence solved the problems this dealer was having without causing him to overspend his monthly budget. Plus, the dealer got the added bonus of seeing his people work their asses off to handle all the traffic and jokingly told me a few months after we had started this process that "nobody in the dealership had any time on their hands to sit around and talk about the glory days."

My final glory-days example comes from a dealership that loved to sit around and relish the day when they ran great ads on television that never showed a price, much less talked about a sale. These ads showed shots of the dealership, shots of the cars and every now and then they went out and filmed footage of the town they were in so their ads could have a real local look and feel to them. It was beyond the thinking in this store to explore the benefit of advertising a price to generate significant traffic. And in hindsight, the real problem was the management seemed to appreciate that while they were running this purely image campaign on television, they were also enjoying the highest SAAR rate in the history of the automotive world from 2004 to 2007. The market was there and the market was buying. On one occasion, the general manager even made a comment to me that people don't need to see an offer. The fact that people know we are here was all that needed to be done. I will admit that we tried advertising the way that this general manager wanted to for a while. He just wouldn't budget to run a price offer, much less promote any type of time-sensitive sales event.

Then, after months of getting our teeth kicked in by the

competition and losing market share, he decided to throw his caution to the wind and run a sales event. The result was an aggressive media schedule with a vertical flight of 300 gross rating points of television backed up by a fully integrated campaign on his website and through email marketing. We ran not just a price, but a price that was $1,000 lower than that of our competitor for the same exact car. This was a point in our relationship that this general manager told me he will never forget. The lift seen by this dealership happened overnight, and it broke through the barrier that "we don't have to price our cars" and we should "just tell the people we are a nice place." It set this dealership on a meteoric rise—they have never gotten off of aggressive marketing to this day.

The world of advertising is changing and changing rapidly. It would be very easy to sit around and rely on the tools and executions that were used in the past to generate traffic, but it isn't that easy anymore and doesn't work that way. The guy who loved direct mail from the 1980s didn't realize that a mailer was more effective when people couldn't go online and shop before coming into the store. Today, the Internet has empowered the shopper to the point they can search and see if what you are saying in the mailer is true or not. It was easier back then and that is what he still wants to hold onto. The managers who didn't want to give up their jingle didn't understand why it worked. They just thought it worked even though only 40 percent of a surveyed audience could not even tell whose jingle it was. Finally, the guy who never wanted to promote a price because his image ads had worked back at a time when the average SAAR was 16 million was easily convinced. When he got his first taste of an aggressive schedule that was backed up by all the elements needed to support it including a super-low price both in TV and on his site, the next day traffic opened his eyes.

While advertising is changing, it is not rocket science. You still are taking a specific amount of money and using it to generate traffic to your dealership. Where this plan can and will get flawed is when you give credence to people like those we have mentioned in this chapter who want to talk about the glory days. They can and will derail a perfectly good plan and end up wasting a whole lot of money because they only remember things to have been a little better than they probably were. And they are certainly not recalling the total market situation at that particular time.

I don't mean to separate older more astute owners and operators from the younger generation in the car business. I'm simply explaining the difference between being able to resist a form of advertising that is out-of-date and only being recommended because it worked for someone back in the glory days. All advertising dollars are an investment in next day traffic, and you can either grow a greater return with a wise investment from those dollars, or they can be wasted. It's your call.

19

MOMENTUM

If you have ever set foot in a dealership and immediately felt that sense of excitement in the air, then you know what I mean when I say that a store can experience "momentum." Not every dealership is capable of it and there is no guarantee that even when you get momentum that you will keep it forever. I have found that momentum is the point at which a great owner or team of managers surround themselves with an incredibly eager team of people armed with a great marketing plan that everyone believes will succeed. When all these factors are combined, you have the opportunity to encounter momentum in a store.

My father, Mike Strong, was also in the automotive advertising industry. Together, both of our careers have spanned five decades, and in that time a lot has changed. When Mike began, television was to dealers what the Internet is now—an unknown new frontier that only a few people could say they had really figured out. At that time there weren't three tiers of automotive advertising. Those levels evolved with the marketing process. While just about everything in this business has changed in some form, I want to examine two principles that still hold true.

The first principle is the Perfect Triangle. It's built by having enough inventory on the ground, the right number of qualified salespeople and a well-conceived advertising plan. These three elements were then and still are the necessary components to grow a dealership's volume and to steal market share. You cannot get by with two out of three on this one. To grow a dealership all pieces must be in place with ownership and management working together inside the triangle. If any piece of this equation is missing or mismanaged, then steady and consistent growth is neither possible nor sustainable. This premise was one of the very first things that my father figured out and it still stands as a pillar in the foundation of how we solve problems in dealerships today.

The second principle, which I touched on earlier, has not changed one bit over the years. Momentum can best be defined as the energy you feel when you walk into a dealership and see sales associates who are eager and moving quickly with purpose. It can initially be seen when you arrive at a dealership and the inventory is not only right but also displayed in immaculate condition. More often than not, momentum is felt more than seen, as the dealership has a constant buzz and endless stream of energy and excitement running through it. Again, not every dealership has momentum and even ones that have it will often lose it. It's a total culmination of all the pieces in an organization working in a synchronized fashion at the same time. It truly can be an impressive and magical thing to see.

The interesting thing about these two principles is that they go hand in hand. You will not experience momentum without the Perfect Triangle functioning on all three sides. Everyone who owns or runs a dealership should already know that success, even if only mediocre, is not possible without the presence of the Perfect Triangle. Momentum is the stuff that legends are made of and what's behind all the stories of dealerships that have destroyed their competitors.

Let's continue by looking at momentum in relationship to the people component. If a dealership has an owner or a general manager who is hard on employees and nobody can stand to be around them, then they will never enjoy momentum. The team must value the leadership at the top and for the right reasons. I have seen a lot of dealerships that will never reach their true potential because the staff doesn't value the opinion or decisions made at the top. Regardless of how great a product you have and how much marketing and promotional power you put behind it, it will fail without proper leadership. This generally occurs when people in higher ranks at dealerships show they are incapable of leadership because they forget too often to appreciate who is doing all the work. The owners and general managers are not greeting customers in the service lane and handling the paperwork in the finance office, it is their staff that does this daily. The manner in which they do it is largely determined by how interested they are in seeing the managers, the owner and ultimately, the dealership succeed. Every store is different with its own set of challenges and opportunities but the one thing that every single dealership has in common is they are all run and managed by people—your team! And in the mind of the customer, your team can either lift your store up or tear it down.

Team communication is critical so that everyone is on the same page, especially with marketing efforts. There are many dealerships where the upper management never tells the sales staff what is going on in regards to marketing. Sales associates have to see the ads on TV, hear them on the radio or have a customer walk up with a mail piece in hand to know what the dealership is currently promoting. If you think this doesn't happen, then think again. I have seen it in some of the largest, most reputable stores in the country. If the staff is not informed of the plan, then the plan never stands a chance of succeeding. Some managers do not want to tell the staff what is going on because they do not want the staff to give their opinion about whether they like the advertising or not. Other managers just forget or do not have the foresight to plan a sales meeting that includes telling the troops what will be bringing the traffic in the door that day. As odd as this may seem, it happens every day all across the country, and thus, millions of marketing dollars spent in hopes of building momentum are wasted every year because there is never any energy and excitement behind the plan.

It's unfortunate that while dealerships are so close to finding their true point of momentum, they will never get there because they just do not know how to inspire and motivate their team. It is imperative to gather the team together and rally the troops at the start of a new campaign or promotion. There will be no sense of excitement when a new direction is started or new incentives clarified unless momentum is harnessed. One example I've seen is when management fails to share relevant information such as, "Yesterday was the highest traffic count in a single day we have ever had on our website." This is momentum motivation for the team that is on the ground to sell the cars. It should inspire them to leave the sales meeting and be primed to conquer the world. Money is a great inspirational tool, but sometimes people need more than money. They need a sense of self-worth that grows when they believe they are an integral part of a winning team. I have often said that a store with momentum is like a freight train that cannot be stopped—these teams are too powerful and have too many tools that other dealerships overlook to ever be derailed. They keep growing and winning in everything they do, and it drives the competition crazy. The best part about freight-train momentum is that even though the competition can see it occurring they can rarely do anything to stop it.

The dealerships that are most capable of building momentum have an owner or general manager who believes the speed of the boss is the speed of the gang, and the staff perceives them as a true leader worth following. This type of leader understands leading by example. He will push himself personally as hard as he will push anyone around him with the goal of being better. When you put this type of person out in front of an organization that has the right inventory, the right amount of sales associates and a marketing plan that covers all angles, you are capable of achieving and sustaining momentum. This type of leader has the ability to groom a team of people who will want to see the top management succeed equally as much as themselves. At this point, success is not only about money but also about winning. Most stores who have momentum know it and show it by taking away share from the other dealers in the market. When everyone on the team has the discipline to perform their daily tasks with a positive attitude, then they have the ability to push the dealership farther than any one individual sitting around interested only in their personal gain. When you generate this type of synergy, then there is no stopping how far you can go and how many millions of dollars can be made. Momentum is centered as much around the people and attitudes in a dealership as anything.

As I alluded to earlier, to create this type of culture is not an easy process, and to keep it going is even tougher. I have seen stores build incredible momentum and then watch it all disappear when one piece of the puzzle is not working right. To achieve monumental success, there has to be a component of marketing included, but a lot of dealerships can succeed just by having a great product and great people who represent the dealership. When you do add in a great advertising plan that generates an endless supply of traffic, you will truly reach utopia—the point when all things are running as smoothly and as perfectly as they can in the car business. If you think this status is only a myth, I can assure you that you are wrong. I have seen these stores first hand and know what it takes to achieve and sustain optimum success.

Because of its delicate nature, momentum can be lost for a myriad of reasons. Momentum is lost when an important person in the dealership leaves to go work somewhere else, or when a product becomes cold to the public. It can leave based on the economy, a war, or any other unforeseen disruption in the retail cycle. Momentum can also disappear with changes in the advertising plan or how the dealership promotes itself. Any minor change to how business is being conducted can unsettle the environment in which momentum existed. Regardless of the circumstance, momentum can be lost in a matter of minutes and it can take years to get it back, especially if you are not careful to sense the turn. And the biggest problem with losing momentum is the amount of money that you have to spend in marketing to get it back. This is a fact: A dealership will not get it back by spending the average dollar per car amount that they are used to spending. It will cost more per car to get it back and even then there is no guarantee that you can regain it immediately.

People who own and run dealerships that are experiencing momentum need to understand that you have to manage the momentum. From the time you achieve it, the management process must be treated as a delicate item and watched constantly. There are no guarantees that you will wake up every day and have great inventory of a tremendous product with enough sales associates who are hungry to conquer the world. These are all critical aspects that have to be worked and refined on an ongoing basis to insure they are consistently firing on all cylinders. Even when you think you have them all tuned-up, you will undoubtedly have a problem arise in one of these areas that can upset the roll you have going.

I have never seen a dealership that kept their momentum forever. It's impossible, and if you play the game long enough, you are going to lose something somewhere that will break your streak. Nobody is capable of maintaining all factors of the Perfect Triangle 365 days a year for years on end. Something is going to happen that affects you somewhere along the way. However, one thing that I have seen is dealerships that lose momentum but quickly regain it. Why? They have been able to assess what went wrong and commit to fixing it quickly to get back on the correct course, and it is truly an art. The ability to adjust and fix what is wrong to regain your momentum is a talent that could be the most valuable skill possessed by anyone in the car business.

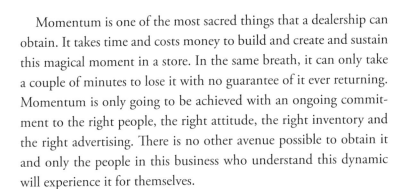

Momentum is one of the most sacred things that a dealership can obtain. It takes time and costs money to build and create and sustain this magical moment in a store. In the same breath, it can only take a couple of minutes to lose it with no guarantee of it ever returning. Momentum is only going to be achieved with an ongoing commitment to the right people, the right attitude, the right inventory and the right advertising. There is no other avenue possible to obtain it and only the people in this business who understand this dynamic will experience it for themselves.

20

10,000 MISSED OPPORTUNITIES

There are tons of missed opportunities on the sales floor because the basic elements in retail car selling are not being followed. Day in and day out I see it in dealerships all across the country without any rhyme or reason. Ultimately, a significant percentage of all advertising dollars that are spent end up wasted, not because dealers do not know what part of their advertising is working, but because they are not utilizing what their advertising is bringing to them. This loss of money adversely effects not only what you will sell in any given week or month, but also the reputation of your store in the mind of the people who decided not to buy from you. There is nothing that you can ever do to change the thinking of someone who has shopped you and decided not to buy, but you *do* have the ability to fix the problem for those who will shop you in the future.

I have seen missed opportunities in many dealerships, even among some of the brightest and best-trained sales teams across the county. I am also amazed to have seen stores where the average monthly unit count for a sales associate is 20 units a month. That was not the high point, mind you, but the average. And it was kept for the entire 12 months of the year. But even when you look at a store with that type of talent level on the floor you still wonder what is happening to all the traffic these great teams aren't closing. Even when a 20-unit team does a phenomenal job at selling, you know they are guilty of missing their fair share of traffic. While a lot of people usually think that traffic is too light or there simply is not enough of it, my experience in every single dealership is the same no matter how good or bad the sales team is. There is always more traffic than you think, and the most overlooked thing is what happens with your traffic after it leaves your store, not while it is in it.

Whether you follow a "road to the sale" training program or subscribe to another industry practice, it doesn't seem to matter in regards to the caliber of people who are being attracted to our industry. Everything as it relates to retail selling comes down to execution. While there are plenty of tools out there to use, very few people actually use them correctly. The dealership averaging 20 units per associate has spent two decades building a team of seasoned and tenured people. They didn't all show up one day and decide they wanted to work for this dealership in this city. It was the dealer who made it his mission to seek out and recruit people who could become career sales associates. He profiled a certain age and maturity level with a very mild manner and level head on their shoulders. Once they were with him, he created a plan to keep them for their career. He wasn't out to find the latest "flash-in-the-pan" who was here today and gone tomorrow, but instead wanted stable and consistent people who would last for decades. This dealer dedicated the majority of his personal efforts to building this team, working tirelessly to get what he wanted. While I have never seen another store devote this time and energy to building a sales force, the one thing that can be done in every store is implementing the proper training program to make your sales team better each day in both their processes and follow-up with their customers.

There are great industry trainers and training programs out there that can also be of benefit to any dealership. I have seen just about all of them, from corporate training programs at work in publically owned stores to outfits like the Joe Verde Group, Grant Cardone, and Jim Ziegler of Ziegler SuperSystems. I have not one bad thing to say about any of the programs or the details that I have seen within their training models. While I do not pretend to be a retail-sales training expert, every one of these programs offers insights that are beneficial. They all work and can help any dealership build better practices and procedures *if* they are followed. To me, that is the biggest problem because they are never followed exactly as they were designed to be. Regardless of how good these trainers and the systems they have created are, they cannot oversee your business every day. At some point, trainers leave stores and the programs go back on the shelf which is where they sadly stay until the trainers come back to the store. In most dealerships programs are implemented with great intentions but the managers and salespeople do not have the discipline to maintain the training and coaching on an ongoing basis. They just do not see how important this piece of the puzzle is and how much better they would be as a salesperson if they actively participated each and every day.

So where does all of this lead us? It takes me to the defining moment when I realized for the first time just how gigantic of a problem properly training salespeople really is for today's dealer. During a year-end marketing meeting with a dealer, we reviewed the ups log traffic counts by month for the first 11 months of the coming year. This dealer, like most, used an electronic tracking system that calculated the number of Internet, phone and floor ups by week for the entire year. He ran a relatively high volume new and used car operation and spent an average of $1.5 million dollars a year on his entire advertising budget. He first added up the columns in his report that showed the year-to-date new and used car sales; then he added the total number of unique ups for the same year-to-date timeframe. When he gave me the numbers, I commented that the amount of ups seemed very high so he double-checked. Again, his calculations confirmed that the numbers were in fact correct because they had all been set up as unique contacts in the CRM (customer retention software) tool that the store uses.

At this point we both started doing the math to subtract the total number of ups from the total sales number. Now picture this, he is using the calculator while I did the math by hand and when we both saw our answers you could have heard a pen drop in that office. Neither one of us said a word or looked at each other for a good 30 seconds because I think we were both trying to make sure we had not made an error in the equation. Finally, when I looked up from my notebook at him, he had a look of utter disbelief and said one word, "How?" I will never forget the silence and feeling that overtook me when I realized the number of unsold ups. The number of ups that had been logged into their system for the year was 9,987. We were stunned that they had already logged in 9,987 missed opportunities for the year, and the year wasn't done!

I rounded the number up to an even 10,000 and felt pretty confident the dealer would have done the same in the next 24 hours if not by the end of the day. His store had received so much traffic that had been logged that it totaled 10,000 missed opportunities to do business in just under a year. There was no way to know how much of the floor traffic didn't get logged but we estimated somewhere between 10 and 15 percent. These numbers did count all sources of traffic including Internet leads, phone calls and floor traffic, and the bottom line was they had received an enormous amount of traffic for the size store they were. Their expected year-end sales volume for new and used cars ended up around 4,000 units and with good gross. They had done a great job selling vehicles that year but the elephant in the room was the fact that they had missed out on 10,000 people who had called, clicked or come by their store and left without buying a vehicle from them.

What was ironic about this experience was a conversation we had a few minutes before calculating these numbers. This dealer specifically asked me if I knew anyone who was really doing a great job at unsold follow-up and what tools were they using. A few people came to mind but I wasn't able to be specific in regard to their processes and systems because I myself was still getting familiar with how they worked. The reason he asked was because he knew his people were terrible at it and he openly admitted the dealership was missing deals because some shoppers were leaving his store and never being contacted again. Although this was not happening to everyone who left without buying, this dealer knew they did not have a solid plan for 30-, 60-, or 90-day unsold prospects. He wanted to find a new training program for his people. He had already looked at a few but wasn't sold on any of them because they all seemed the same, and he knew his people were ultimately going to have to buy into the chosen process in order for it to work.

After we saw the numbers and all the missed opportunity, the dealer discovered what his number one priority was for the upcoming year. To this dealer's credit, he is a savvy operator who is active in the daily operations of his dealership. But even while being so close to all aspects of his business, he never dreamed that they were letting this many people get away—a problem compounded by having a poor system for follow-up. We also talked about where and how we were going to increase his budget to keep up with the growing market for the next year because the sales projections and his own dealership projections were up double-digit percentages from the previous years. After the revelation of what was happening with the number of unsold customers, we both agreed that it wasn't going to be beneficial to increase our advertising spend when that level of opportunity was already being missed on an annual basis.

We saw that if the dealership focused on training its people to be better with the traffic they were getting, then they could sell more cars while spending the same amount of money. Extra dollars could go into a training budget, an element that was clearly needed. I respect this dealer and the decision to not follow the popular industry stance of some people who say, "If you get us the traffic, then we will close them." I realize it is ultimately the job of the marketing company, and every vendor you use, to supply you with traffic, but if you think that your people are good enough to close every single up that walks through your door, then you have another thing coming. Nobody is that good. Without a doubt, a certain percentage of shoppers you see every day, whether in-store, online or on the phone, simply are not ready to buy. The better the processes you develop for your follow-up with these people are, the more sales you will reap from them.

Missed opportunities, especially 10,000, are a lot for any dealership and it takes a smart person like this dealer to calculate how much waste is coming, not as a result of advertising but from the sales process. The Internet buying and selling process has added a whole new dimension to the traffic counts that a store receives in a given month. This is not talking about unique web traffic, but actual justified leads that come to you from your website or those who are calling you after looking on your website. Even while the market is not as large as in previous years, dealerships are getting more traffic, more leads and more opportunities because customers now have more ways to shop. Some dealerships excel at how they follow-up with online leads but still fall short when it comes to staying in front of the leads generated off the floor. Other stores do great with somebody walking in the front door, but cannot handle a structured Internet follow-up process. And while some stores seemingly have all angles covered, the people directly involved with doing the follow-up may be the ones who let the process fail. There are plenty of different ways that it can fail, and it is failing in dealerships everywhere you look.

Whether your salespeople average 20 or eight units a person is irrelevant. Every store has customers who shop who are not ready to buy in that very moment. These customers are ultimately going to buy something from somewhere, and if you continue to operate with a poorly executed follow-up system, then chances are pretty good that they are not going to buy from you. The dealerships with the best follow-up systems and people diligently working the systems will sell a greater share of these people for one reason—they stay in front of them.

Every dealership will have missed opportunities and there will always be oversights if the proper processes are not followed by your sales staff. As mind-boggling as it seems, things do sometimes go wrong, even when you have the right process in place. You have to do the best you can to minimize the amount of people who come to your dealership through advertising but do not buy because of weak processes. They slip through possibly because of your people or your process, but in the end, something is flawed and you missed the opportunity to do business because of it. No dealership is perfect and no sales team is faultless, which is why you must be able to evaluate how well you are doing with unsold customers. Failure in monitoring the numbers that are getting away ensures you will never be taking full advantage of the advertising plan and what it is generating.

Advertising dollars for a dealership are an investment in traffic. Those dollars will either yield a lesser or a greater return-on-investment for the dealership based on what was behind the decisions in placing the media and what was driving the creative. What an impact it was on me when I first did the math and realized that I was sitting in a store that had squandered 10,000 missed opportunities in a year's time. I have never met anyone who can fix what happened yesterday but I believe with all the confidence in the world that a smart person can fix what happens tomorrow. Our dealer took this problem in his store and tackled it head-on because he knew that these missed opportunities could be attributed to the strength of his own store's follow-up skills. He accepted and identified the problem and has taken steps every day since that day of discovery to fix it and guarantee it never gets out of control again.

I have told dealers before that I have never met a store that couldn't be fixed by creating enough traffic. But after this experience, and seeing the real impact on a dealer of learning that he had 10,000 missed opportunities over the course of a year in which he spent well over one million dollars on advertising, I have altered that saying. Now I tell people I never met a store that couldn't be fixed by creating enough traffic and one that couldn't be made incredible if it has the right sales process to back it up. Easier said than done, but the sooner you get your dealership on a solid follow-up foundation the sooner your store will take off toward the next level.

21

A TERRIBLE THING HAPPENS WITHOUT PROMOTION...NOTHING

P.T. Barnum was perhaps the greatest promoter who ever lived and this quote of his was at the very core of his philosophy, "A terrible thing happens without promotion...NOTHING!" He believed that if you are not promoting then you have no hope of drawing a big crowd. The parallel to our industry is no chance of generating traffic. Keep in mind, when Barnum began there were no case studies or business books on how to be a successful promoter. What he discovered, he did on his own through an extensive amount of trial and error. His belief was that you had to truly capture a person's imagination to draw their attention to what you were trying to sell. So his just wasn't a circus but The Greatest Show on Earth. Without a doubt, he used a lot of tricks and gimmicks to attract a crowd but he was always promoting his shows through whatever means necessary to fill the seats. Sound familiar? Regardless of what one may think of some of the tactics that he used, nobody can disagree with his success and what he was able to create and sustain.

I believe in and have built a marketing model based off of three types of traffic for automotive dealerships all across the country for all different brands: natural traffic, owner body traffic, and created traffic. If you decided that you were not going to aggressively promote your business to the public for whatever reason, you would still see natural and owner body traffic, but you would never have the ability to attract people beyond those two and enjoy created traffic. Created traffic is the desired end result of just about all of your marketing efforts because in most cases you are expending money and effort to *create* a customer out of someone who currently is not a customer and most likely not going to be in the future. The final piece in the three types of traffic relies strictly on promotion, and if you do not have it then you are going to end up with what P.T. Barnum clearly understood—nothing!

I realize there are dealerships that have been successful with very little advertising over the years. There are also dealerships that have created incredible market awareness and can now reduce advertising spending and still remain effective. But for a dealership to create and maintain the momentum, they are going to have to remain consistently aggressive with their advertising. As a result, more created traffic will grow year after year. We discussed the variables that can cause disruption to a dealership's business from the economy to gas prices, the threat of war or a natural disaster. These factors and others are why even flirting with the thought of not having enough traffic should be something that a dealer or general manager doesn't even let enter their stream of consciousness.

Traffic can fix any problem in any dealership, so there is no reason why you would not want to get absolutely as much of it as you can, even if your processes for handling unsold customers are not 100 percent. Traffic comes in many different ways through all types of mass media and digital media outlets as discussed previously, but do not ever fall victim to thinking that you can sustain without it. If your salespeople and managers did everything they were supposed to without being asked, then yes, you could think about not promoting. If your competitors all decided that they would not promote their business either, then yes, you can think about not promoting. When your manufacturer rep walks in and says they have a blank check and are going to spend all the money in the world in your market, then yes, you can think about not promoting. But you and I both know that these things are never going to happen. So you can never think that you can survive and prosper from not promoting, much less attempt it.

How you promote and what you are going to promote are questions that very few people can answer. Dealers and general managers are responsible for running the departments that make up a dealership. On top of managing new cars, used cars, parts, service, finance and occasionally collision centers, you are going to need help to move forward with a great marketing plan. True, the person in charge of the store will have as good an idea as anyone regarding what type of promotions will work, but either a specialized marketing company or promotional expert is going to be required to come up with and execute all the day-to-day details that are required to realize success. I have found that coming up with a message that gives the consumer a reason to buy, a reason to buy today, and a reason to buy from this particular dealership is where dealerships need the help of a professional. It is flawed thinking of the worst kind to assume that effective promotional messages can be created as well as executed by the current team inside the dealership. There are simply not enough hours in the day or detail-driven experience for the team primarily responsible for selling and servicing the cars to allow for this. I value and respect the managers with great insight and market-based information but creating a promotional message cannot be left up to them. Having managers in total control of advertising decisions is the equivalent of having advertising people come into a dealership to sell cars and manage the process. It just doesn't work like that because in today's 720 degrees of marketing, an entirely different set of skills are necessary.

The last and final piece for effective promoting is consistency. The word "consistent" has been used many times in this book and I believe if P.T. Barnum was alive today, he would rework his quote as follows, "A terrible thing happens without promotion on a consistent basis—nothing! And nothing can be a very long time." I find myself telling people on a regular basis that this is a marathon, not a sprint. This is probably more true to the car business than any other industry out there. Too many times, an advertising and promotional strategy gets changed at the drop of a hat when something doesn't go right on the sales side of the business. This is why it takes the planning abilities of someone who knows the marketing world *and* the dealership inside and out to prepare the right kind of promotion to not only make the customers respond but make the people in the dealership respond as well. When the people inside the dealership buy-in because they have been motivated and educated as to why the advertisement will work, then that promotion stands a much better chance for succeeding.

In this business, you are measured as a winner or a loser every single month and with the beginning of a new month, the whole game starts back over again. If a store is not doing well, the factory looks at the dealer. If the sales are not where they need to be, the dealer looks at the sales department. If the store is not handling enough volume in the service business, then the dealer looks at the service department. Too many times, if advertising has not delivered the desired amount of traffic in a month, it gets stopped or changed without examining or understanding why. Don't get me wrong, advertising by design exists for the sole purpose of generating next day traffic, but it always has to be measured and compared to what is happening in the rest of the market and with your competition. Gains in market share against other dealers as well as vehicle brands do take time. Sometimes growth comes slowly. But the best thing about these gains is that even if they are slow in coming, by the time you start to notice them, everyone else does too.

Being consistent with your advertising dictates that you give that particular program a reasonable amount of time to be tested before changing it in any way. Do not expect to start a new marketing plan and in five days experience a total turnaround. You may have seen more traffic and sold more cars in those five days but the long-term effects of the campaign sometimes take weeks, months or even years to really see the benefit of what has been gained through stable marketing and advertising. Turnaround questions like, "How long until this starts to work?" or "How long until we see some results?" are what I get asked the most by dealers. My answer always addresses the pivotal point: You will start to see and feel a new sense of momentum from created traffic as soon as a new campaign starts to run, but it may take you several months before you really start to convert the effects of this new traffic into noticeable sales gains. I have experienced the gamut of turnarounds in dealerships going through promotional changes with some as little as 30 days and others taking as long as three years before everything clicked. Ultimately, it depends on the speed and attitude of the dealership and the depth to which they embrace the promotion.

There are so many different ways in which you can promote. There are even more things that you can choose to say within your promotional message to create traffic. This is why you have so many people knocking on your door to sell you on their ideas. This is why every dealership must have a promotional plan in place and resolve that they are going to follow the plan and work the plan as it has been created. Set your idea-consideration standards to the highest because the difference between, "I think this will work" and "I know this works and here is why" is a tough lesson. Take this entire subject and boil it down to the simplest form: If you are not promoting, you do not stand a chance against dealers that are aggressively promoting. The market share will not all go away tomorrow for the dealer who isn't promoting, but over time it is going to erode and then disappear. This is not a two-sided coin. The dealer who promotes the most consistently with the best message will win by enjoying the most Created Traffic while the non-promoters are getting what they asked for—nothing!

Next day traffic in your dealership is more than a goal, it is your livelihood. I hold the men and women of this industry in the highest esteem because the victory won today is just that, and tomorrow you prove yourself again on a battlefield that is undergoing constant change. My privilege has been to learn from so many who have been in the trenches and my desire is that this book provides you with insights to succeed in your endeavor. I thank you for the opportunity to stand beside you in the relentless pursuit of excellence.